Open for Debate

Religious
Fundamentalism

Ron Fridell

New York

Thanks to Martin E. Marty,
Fairfax M. Cone Distinguished Service Professor Emeritus,
Divinity School, University of Chicago,
for his thoughtful review of the manuscript.

Marshall Cavendish Benchmark
99 White Plains Road
Tarrytown, NY 10591
www.marshallcavendish.us

Library of Congress Cataloging-in-Publication Data

Fridell, Ron.
Religious fundamentalism / by Ron Fridell.
p. cm. — (Open for debate)
Includes bibliographical references and index.
ISBN 978-0-7614-2945-6
1. Religious fundamentalism—Juvenile literature. I. Title.
BL238.F76 2009
200.9'04—dc22
2008000364

Photo research by Lindsay Aveilhe and Linda Sykes/
Linda Sykes Photo Research, Hilton Head, SC

Cover photos: Alan Powdrill/Taxi/Getty Images: front cover (left)
Majid/Getty Images: front cover (right)

The photographs in this book are used by permission and through the courtesy of:
Alan Powdrill/Taxi/Getty Images: 1 (left); Majid/Getty Images: 1 (right); Time and Life
Pictures/Getty Images: 4, 29; Claudia Kunin/Corbis: 11; Museo di San Marco dell'
Angelico, Florence, Italy/Giraudon/The Bridgeman Art Library: 20; Dennis Kitchen/Stone/
Getty Images: 25; Peter Yates/Corbis: 36; Kurt Stier/Corbis: 42; AFP/Getty Images: 44;
Win McNamee/Reuters/Corbis: 47; Reuters/Corbis: 57, 62; Kazuyoshi Nomachi/Corbis:
68; Andrew Holbrooke/Corbis: 79; Getty Images: 85; University Library Istanbul, Turkey/
The Bridgeman Art Library: 89; AFP/Getty Images: 96; Vincent Kessler/Reuters/Corbis: 111.

Publisher: Michelle Bisson
Art Director: Anahid Hamparian
Series Designer: Sonia Chaghatzbanian

Printed in Malaysia
1 3 5 6 4 2

Contents

This 1966 *Time* magazine cover did not ask whether God was literally, physically dead. It asked whether people still saw God as a real, guiding source of moral values in their lives.

1
How Fundamentalists See the World

IS GOD DEAD?

The question appeared in dark red letters on a stark black background on the cover of *Time* magazine, April 8, 1966. The article inside, titled "Toward a Hidden God," presented the opinions of Christian theologians who feared that the "death of God" had come to the United States.

The conclusions of these religious men were disturbing: God was virtually invisible in public life, and religion was all but dead. The article told of doubting and bewildered believers who had "quietly abandoned all but token allegiance to the churches," and a God who no longer touched their emotions or engaged their minds.

Four decades later an article in the same magazine announced that religion had made an unexpected comeback, not just in the United States but around the world. In the December 21, 2006, issue of *Time*, author and columnist Andrew Sullivan wrote, "Not only did it arrive as the most powerful cultural force of the new millennium, it also came in a particular guise [identity]. It was a fundamentalist version of faith that was triumphant."

Back to the Roots

What exactly is this potent brand of faith? Fundamentalism is not a mainstream religion, such as Judaism, Methodism, Catholicism, or Islam. It is not a separate religion at all. Fundamentalism is a branch of an existing faith. Most of the world's mainstream religions have fundamentalist branches.

Each branch consists of discontented believers who strongly disagree with what the mainstream church has become. To their way of thinking, the faith as practiced by most people is no longer authentic. It has lost contact with its vital traditions and principles, its fundamental roots. And so these discontents have broken away from the mainstream faith to form their own fundamentalist branch housed in their own church, committed to returning to those roots.

Religious fundamentalists are idealists involved in a movement to bring about change. They see their society the way they see the mainstream church: in terms of how it might be changed for the better. This idealism is only one part of their worldview.

Five Beliefs

Defining the fundamentalist worldview is no simple matter. Each of the world's many fundamentalist groups has its own unique way of looking at the world. But five beliefs that most groups share in some form give a general idea of what fundamentalism is all about. These beliefs apply especially to the two dominant forms of religious fundamentalism at work in the world today: Christian and Islamic.

The first belief: the world is a battleground. The forces of Good, commanded by a loving but wrathful superhuman God, battle the forces of Evil, led by Satan, a supernatural being relentlessly at work on Earth corrupting souls. The battles take place in the invisible spiritual realm as well as the physical world. Angels and demons, invisible to humans, take part in the conflict, which is destined to last until Christ returns to Earth in fleshly form and history itself comes to a devastating, catastrophic, earthshaking halt. Millions of people will be slaughtered, but the forces of Good will prevail.

The second belief: The religion's divinely inspired writings, or scripture, reveal the Creator's truths. For Christians it's the Holy Bible, the Old and New Testaments. For Muslims it's the Quran (sometimes spelled *Qur'an* or *Koran*). Most nonfundamentalist believers tend to view these writings as mixtures of fact, allegory, parable, and poetry. But to fundamentalists, each and every word of scripture is literally true and accurate, both scientifically and historically.

The third belief: Fundamentalists must be true believers, maintaining strict moral values and never doubting or questioning their faith, the one and only true faith on Earth. They must surrender to the Creator completely and allow his will alone, as interpreted by church leaders, to guide their thoughts and actions.

The fourth belief: Secularism, or modernism, is a corrupt worldview that rejects religious traditions and moral values in terms of human traditions and moral values. Secularism is humanity's deliberate, sinful revolt against God. As a result, behaviors such as homosexuality, abortion, and gambling are legal. Believers must fight secularism wherever they find it, whether in government, culture, or mainstream religions.

The fifth belief: God rewards believers' faith with eternity in Heaven. The rest, the unsaved, are condemned to the fires of Hell. Believers must work to convert the unsaved to their fundamentalist faith. They must also keep striving to transform secular society until it accurately reflects the faith's strict moral values.

The Critics

What about nonfundamentalists? How do they feel about secularism? R. Scott Appleby is associate professor of history at Notre Dame University, and Martin E. Marty is professor of the History of Modern Christianity at the University of Chicago. The two have been instrumental in putting together *The Fundamentalism Project*, a scholarly study of fundamentalism worldwide. In a magazine interview, Appleby observed that many nonfundamentalists are also concerned about AIDS, drug abuse, rising divorce rates, and other modern problems.

But fundamentalists' concerns are more passionate and personal, Appleby explained. "They interpret these events not as coincidences or accidental but as a kind of conspiracy of the opponents of religion. . . . They see this as a concerted effort by unbelievers to displace God's natural order." And so fundamentalists see themselves as virtuous soldiers in a global war of Good against Evil.

This warlike attitude draws sharp criticism from non-fundamentalists who oppose the radical remaking of society according to a worldview they do not share. Besides moderate and liberal-minded members of mainstream religions, critics of fundamentalism include agnostics—those who doubt the existence of God—and atheists, who do not believe in God at all. Critics also include political leaders, educators, historians, scientists, scholars, authors, and journalists. What follows is an examination of the clash between religious fundamentalists and their critics, focusing on Christian and Islamic fundamentalism.

2
Christian Fundamentalism

Some five hundred years ago many members of the Catholic religion had become profoundly disenchanted with their faith. In their eyes Catholicism had become a corrupt institution. For example, there was the widespread practice of selling "indulgences." An indulgence was a note that went from the Church directly to God. Catholic clergymen would issue these messages to God in exchange for a gift of money to the Church. In the note, the clergyman would put in a good word for the giver of the gift. With an indulgence, the giver—or a loved one who had died—stood a better chance of getting into Heaven because he or she had given money to the Church. Only Catholic clergymen could issue indulgences, the Church proclaimed, because only they could put believers in direct contact with God.

The more Catholic clergymen used the profits from indulgences for their personal benefit, the richer and more powerful they became—and the more protest they stirred up. The word *protest* is the root of *Protestant*. Catholic protesters took action by forming a powerful movement to reform the Church.

But this protest movement went beyond reform. It led to reformation—the creation of new Protestant religions based on the belief that individuals could make direct contact with God without the help of clergy.

Fundamental Questions

During the next four hundred years, Christianity came to include not only Catholicism but dozens of other Protestant religions, such as Lutheran, Baptist, Methodist, and Presbyterian. Then, during the early years of the twentieth century, another religious protest movement arose. More and more conservative Protestants had grown dissatisfied with their faith. They felt it was losing out to secularism as an influence in American life.

Conservative clergymen and churchgoers expressed their dissatisfaction with a series of booklets entitled *The Fundamentals: A Testimony to the Truth*. From this title came the term *fundamentalism*, which called upon Protestant believers to stand up and fight for a return to the roots of their religion, to the essential beliefs that must always serve as the basis for true Christianity. Among these sacred beliefs were: that Jesus Christ was not conceived as other humans are, but that his mother, Mary, was a virgin; that Jesus is God in fleshly form; that the Bible is God's word; and that Christ will return to Earth to reward the faithful, punish unbelievers, and put an end to human history.

Liberal-minded Protestants did not see these sacred beliefs the same way that fundamentalists saw them. In 1922 a well-known Presbyterian minister delivered a sermon contrasting the attitudes of liberal and fundamentalist believers. His name was Harry Emerson Fosdick and his sermon was titled, "Shall the Fundamentalists Win?"

FUNDAMENTALISTS AND OTHER CONSERVATIVE CHRISTIANS BELIEVE THAT JESUS CHRIST WAS CRUCIFIED—EXECUTED BY HAVING HIS HANDS AND FEET NAILED TO A CROSS—AND THAT THREE DAYS LATER HE ROSE FROM THE DEAD AND ASCENDED INTO HEAVEN.

Fosdick's sermon focused on the fundamentalists' insistence that anyone who challenged these sacred beliefs lost the right to be called a true Christian. "This is a free country," Fosdick responded, "and anybody has a right to hold these opinions or any others if he is sincerely convinced of them. The question is—Has anybody a right to deny the Christian name to those who differ with him on such points and to shut against them the doors of the Christian fellowship?"

In other words, must a person be a fundamentalist Christian to be considered a Christian at all? The liberal-minded Fosdick said no, while fundamentalists said yes, absolutely. The controversy continues today. Dozens of fundamental questions about the nature of Christianity are being discussed in churches and in mass media nationwide. Here are some of those questions and the positions taken by the opposing sides.

What Makes a True Christian?

Fundamentalists insist that a true Christian must be born again. They cite Jesus's words in the New Testament, John 3:3: "Truly, truly, I say to you, unless one is born again he cannot see the kingdom of God" (*New American Standard Bible*).

Being born again means accepting Jesus Christ as one's personal savior. When this happens, the believer is spiritually reborn as a brand new human being—saved. Born-again Christians are certain they are saved: rescued from the punishments of Hell and bound for Heaven. They believe that their faith in Jesus Christ has saved them, that this faith alone guarantees them eternal life in Paradise.

But many nonfundamentalist Christians also consider themselves born again. What sets fundamentalists apart from others who consider themselves born again? One factor is their attitude toward the supernatural. While many nonfundamentalist Christians also believe in God, Satan, angels, and demons, fundamentalists are more insistent about their literal reality. To a fundamentalist, God, Satan, angels, and demons are without question actual, literal beings. Harold Brown of Trinity Evangelical Divinity School in Deerfield, Illinois, expressed this fundamentalist position when he wrote that Satan is "a real and powerful adversary, one who is determined to do us as much harm as he can." But is Satan a danger to a true born-again believer? "[E]ven those who know the Bible and seek to walk by faith are not beyond Satan's attacks," Brown wrote. "Satan will do all he can to make us doubt God's love and drive us to disillusionment, depression, and if possible, despair."

Critics on Satan and God

One reason that moderate and liberal Christians oppose fundamentalists is their differing views on Satan and God. Bruce Bawer is an essayist and author who often writes about religious matters. He is also a liberal Christian. Bawer sees Satan not as a real, actual being but as "a metaphor for the potential for evil that exists in each person, Christian or otherwise." Evil cannot be conquered in any battle, spiritual or otherwise. Evil cannot be eliminated from the world, Bawer writes, because it is within us all. It is up to each person to recognize this potential for evil within and resist it.

Critics also object to the way fundamentalists tend to view God. When liberal and moderate Christians think of the Creator, they typically picture the kind and loving God of the New Testament, the part of the Bible devoted to Jesus, the Son of God, and his teachings. In the Book of Matthew, for instance, when Jesus was asked about the

A Momentous Change

Britt Williams describes the moment that he was converted and became a born-again Christian. Today he is Pastor Britt Williams, a fundamentalist Protestant minister.

> One February night in 1987, while alone at home and tormented with conviction, I became keenly aware of my awful sinfulness and brazen rebellion against a loving and holy God. Desperate in spirit, I knelt in my bedroom and cried out to God. I sensed God's presence and knew He demanded a full surrender of my life. For many months I had *"counted the cost"* of discipleship but it was at this defining moment that I was brought to my spiritual breakpoint. I perceived that God was confronting me with an ultimatum—*it was now, or perhaps never.* Like every true disciple before me, I am glad to report that by God's divine grace, I was able to lay down my life that night and follow the Master.

In an e-mail interview, Williams was asked if all born-again conversions take place this way, in a single moment in time. Or do they sometimes take place slowly, over weeks or even longer? Williams answered:

> Most Protestants (and as far as I know, nearly all fundamentalists) believe that actual conversion . . . takes place in a moment, namely, when any sinner repents and exercises faith in the finished work of Christ. However, the preparatory work referred to in the Bible as *"conviction"* (that works to draw men to Jesus) will predate conversion and may indeed last for an extended period of time.

Williams' ministry, headquartered in Baton Rouge, Louisiana, is known as Consuming Fire Fellowship. It is an open-air/street ministry, with preaching taking place "in front of barrooms, bus stations, rock concerts, on college campuses, in town squares, and just about anywhere and everywhere people congregate as the Lord leads."

single greatest law, this was his reply: "Thou shalt love the Lord thy God with all thy heart, and with all thy soul, and with all thy mind. This is the first and great commandment. And the second is like unto it, Thou shalt love thy neighbour as thyself. On these two commandments hang all the law and the prophets" (Matthew 22:37–40, *King James Version*).

But, critics say, fundamentalists tend to focus on the God of the Old Testament, the part of the Bible written before the birth of Jesus. This Old Testament God tends to be angry and vengeful. In this passage from the Book of Zephaniah, for example, God proclaims: "For my decision is to gather nations, to assemble kingdoms, to pour out upon them my indignation, all my burning anger; for all the earth will be devoured by the fire of my zeal" (Zephaniah 3:8, *New American Standard Bible*).

Why do fundamentalists tend to de-emphasize the loving Jesus of the New Testament? Because Jesus's message of nonviolence does not reflect their view of life as an ongoing battle between the forces of good and evil. "In America right now, millions of children are taught by their [fundamentalist] Christian parents and ministers to revere a God of wrath," Bawer writes.

Since atheists do not believe in God, they are not in favor of any organized religion based on a belief in the supernatural, and that includes all forms of fundamentalism. When it comes to God, Satan, angels, demons, and the battle between Good and Evil, atheists say no to all of it. Author and journalist Susan Jacoby writes, "All belief in the supernatural; i.e., that which contradicts the laws of nature, is irrational by definition." And essayist and author Christopher Hitchens writes, "Our belief is not a belief. Our principles are not a faith. We do not rely solely upon science and reason . . . but we distrust anything that contradicts science or outrages reason."

Is the Bible Literally God's Truth?

For Christians, the Bible is the most authoritative source on their religion. But for fundamentalist Christians, the Bible is more than just authoritative—it is the one and only truly reliable source of knowledge on Earth. The Southern Baptist Convention is the United States's largest Protestant fundamentalist group. On its Web site, the group writes, "The Holy Bible was written by men divinely inspired and is God's revelation of Himself to man. It is a perfect treasure of divine instruction. It has God for its author, salvation for its end, and truth, without any mixture of error, for its matter."

To fundamentalists, all sixty-six books of the Bible are scientifically and historically accurate. For example, when the Old Testament Book of Genesis says that God created the Earth and all living things in six twenty-four-hour days, it means exactly that. It is a revealed truth, a fact revealed by God. Scientists may present evidence to the contrary. They may present evidence that the planet Earth is actually billions of years old and that living things have evolved slowly through all those years. But that evidence is false and misleading, fundamentalists believe, since it contradicts God's absolute and unchanging truth. The Bible is literally—historically and scientifically—accurate in all ways. Here, evolutionary biologist and author Richard Dawkins sums up the fundamentalist attitude toward scripture:

> **Fundamentalists know they are right because they have read the truth in a holy book and they know, in advance, that nothing will budge them from their belief. The truth of the holy book is an axiom [an unproven assumption], not the end product of a**

17

process of reasoning. The book is true, and if the evidence seems to contradict it, it is the evidence that must be thrown out, not the book.

Interpreting the Bible

Many nonfundamentalist Christians agree that the Bible is divinely inspired, but they don't think that it is accurate in every detail, that it contains the whole of God's truth. Baptist minister Rowland Croucher, founding director of John Mark Ministries in Australia, writes: "The Bible is God's written revelation of his will for us. Like Jesus, the living Word of God, the Scriptures are both divine and human documents. The Bible is the final authority for all our beliefs and practices. But we interpret the Bible humbly, not dogmatically, because 'the Lord has yet more light and truth to break forth from his holy Word.'"

Croucher believes that God's truth is not something humans can know. The best that people can hope to do is read the Bible carefully, interpret what they find there for themselves, and arrive at their own understanding.

Fosdick took a more openly critical stand in "Shall the Fundamentalists Win?" Speaking of their belief that everything in the Bible is infallible, including all "scientific opinions, medical theories, historical judgments, as well as spiritual insight," he said: "That is one idea of the Bible's inspiration. But side by side with those who hold it, lovers of the Book as much as they, are multitudes of people who never think about the Bible so. Indeed, that static and mechanical theory of inspiration seems to them a positive peril to the spiritual life."

By "static and mechanical theory of inspiration," Fosdick means that God would not be so simple of mind as to dictate the sum total of his knowledge to a few men, who then transcribed it all neatly into what we now know as the Bible. And God's knowledge could not be so transparent and unchanging that humans could ever know it completely.

And surely everything in the Bible cannot be taken as literally true, critics insist. After all, the Old Testament is full of events that no rational person could believe. Moses turns the Nile River to blood and parts the waters of the Red Sea. Joshua stops the sun at noontime. Samson kills one thousand men with the jawbone of an ass. And so on. Bawer writes that taking the Bible literally forces people to struggle to believe things "that plainly and directly contradict the facts of observable reality, even though one does not admit the contradiction to others and tries not to admit it even to oneself."

Then there are those Christians who do not see the Bible as holy scripture, divinely inspired. To them it is literature, a wide-ranging collection of ancient fables, myths, folktales, poems, letters, parables, and allegories assembled by a number of different people over time. Together, this collection of literature is meant to help explain how the world got to be as it is and how people ought to relate to nature and to one another. The Bible's considerable wisdom and insight is a matter of personal interpretation, not a matter of fact.

Is the Future Set in Stone?

For Christian fundamentalists, the future has already been decided by God, including the final chapter of human history, which is written out in The Revelation of St. John the Divine, the last book of the New Testament. Fundamentalists call this final chapter the End Times. There are different interpretations of the events that make up the End Times, but most go something like this:

First comes the Rapture, when all believers who have

died in the past will rise from their graves and, along with all living believers, ascend into Paradise, leaving the rest of humanity behind. Pastor John Hagee of the Cornerstone Church in San Antonio, Texas, proclaims that "All over the Earth, graves will explode as the occupants soar into the heavens."

Then comes the Great Tribulation, a seven-year period of terrible suffering. The forces of Satan, commanded by an evil being known as the Antichrist, persecute and kill all who refuse to worship him. There is war and plague. The oceans dry up. Rivers turn to blood. People are scorched with fire from the sun.

THIS DETAIL FROM A FIFTEENTH-CENTURY PAINTING BY ITALIAN ARTIST FRA ANGELICO SHOWS SATAN DEVOURING THE DAMNED, WHO, ACCORDING TO THE BOOK OF REVELATION, WILL BE SENT TO HELL BY CHRIST ON JUDGMENT DAY.

Then Christ returns on a sea of heavenly clouds to set up his earthly kingdom. He destroys the Antichrist and his followers and takes Satan prisoner. Christ then reigns peacefully over Earth for the next thousand years. Then comes Judgment Day, when Christ sends the remaining unsaved into a punishing lake of fire, and human history comes to an end.

When will the End Times occur? Fundamentalists say that only God knows for sure, but they remain on the lookout for signs of its approach. Reverend Pat Robertson is a well-known and influential fundamentalist preacher, head of television's Christian Broadcasting Network (CBN). In October 2005, Robertson pointed out how several hurricanes had recently struck the United States, and that in December 2004 a catastrophic earthquake in Southeast Asia had brought forth a devastating tsunami that claimed thousands of lives. When Robertson was asked whether these were signs of the approach of the End Times, he replied: "It's possible. I don't have any special revelation to say it is but the Bible does indicate such a time will happen in the end of time. And could this be it? It might be."

But the End Times never will arrive, critics insist, because human history is not already written out by God. History unfolds as a succession of acts of human nature and the environment, not the pronouncements of a supernatural being. Nonfundamentalists tend to see this biblical view of history as far-fetched, cruel, and horrifying. But fundamentalists see it as inevitable, fair, and satisfying, with a just and wrathful God giving all people on earth exactly what they deserve.

3
Faith versus Doubt

When fundamentalists look at the world outside their church and its community of believers, they typically see a perplexing place full of people who appear to be living their lives without guidance, empty of purpose, and devoid of God's moral values. George Marsden, religious historian and professor of history at the University of Notre Dame, writes: "In typical fundamentalist churches people . . . value fundamentalist discipline. Those who feel disoriented by the mobility and impersonality and plethora of choices of contemporary life are attracted to the stability of a close-knit community with clear values and unambiguous sources of authority." Fundamentalists crave the stability that their faith gives them: the gift of certainty in an uncertain world.

Does Faith Leave Room for Doubt?

In return for this certainty, fundamentalists must be true believers. They must surrender their will to God. When it comes to their religion, they have to accept everything on faith—blind faith that neither questions nor argues nor wonders nor doubts.

For fundamentalist believers, faith comes from God and doubt comes from Satan. Doubting one's religion leads believers away from proper doctrine, the religion's rock-solid system of beliefs, and draws them toward the perils of personal judgment. For true believers, private opinions and desires can only drive a wedge between them and the truth of the Bible.

Truth comes from the Creator. God is the only source of truth about what is good and what is evil, what is right and what is wrong. When doubting believers stop listening to God and church leaders and start making their own moral judgments, they become their own personal God operating under their own moral code with their own ideas about right and wrong. And that leads to moral relativism—moral anarchy, with everyone doing whatever they wish. When mainstream churches tell people that God loves us no matter what we say or do, they are promoting moral relativism. When it comes to right and wrong, fundamentalists say, believers must rely strictly on the Bible and the advice and instruction of church leaders. Doubt has no good place in the mind of a true believer.

Nonfundamentalists on Faith and Doubt

Author Christopher Hitchens, an avowed atheist, strongly objects to the idea that morality comes only from religion. He writes, "[Atheists] believe with certainty that an ethical life can be lived without religion." In fact, Hitchens insists, the concept of right and wrong thought and action did not originate with religions at all. The opposite is true. Religions got their moral standards from everyday living. Secular—nonreligious—morality goes back thousands of years. According to the early Greek philosopher Socrates, people should not depend on a god or gods for their moral code. They should figure out for themselves the difference between right and wrong behavior and live with that moral code in mind. Atheists agree with Socrates. Morality is available to all through their own minds and consciences, through reason. This way of thinking has been labeled atheistic humanism or secular humanism, a rejection of the supernatural when it comes to making moral and ethical decisions.

As for doubt, nonfundamentalist believers typically find it both natural and indispensable. For one thing, a person who is without doubt is a person whose mind is closed. Bruce Bawer writes that "the mind is a gift of God and . . . God wants us to think for ourselves, to follow our consciences, to ask questions, and to listen for his still, small voice."

By "still, small voice," a quote from the Bible (1 Kings 19:12), Bawer means an inner thought, a quiet inspiration that sets the doubting listener in the right direction. Believers should not be afraid to make their own decisions in cooperation with their faith. Faith should influence behavior but not dictate it. Conscience and faith should be partners.

Mark C. Taylor, head of the Department of Religion at Columbia University in New York, regularly sees a fundamentalist attitude toward doubt in his classroom. Taylor is a liberal Christian whose classes are designed to raise doubts in students' minds about faith and morality, and he challenges them to struggle with those doubts. "A growing number of religiously correct [fundamentalist-minded] students consider this challenge a direct assault on their faith," Taylor writes. "Yet the task of thinking and teaching, especially in an age of emergent fundamentalisms, is to cultivate a faith in doubt that calls into question every certainty."

FUNDAMENTALISM LEAVES NO ROOM FOR QUESTION OR DOUBT.
ANGELS AND DEMONS MAY BE INVISIBLE, BUT FOR THE TRUE
BELIEVER, THEY ARE ABSOLUTELY REAL.

Their close-minded attitude puts fundamentalists at odds with those who look to secular science and history for their worldview. Christian fundamentalists must believe that God created everything in six twenty-four-hour days, for example, even though this belief contradicts solid scientific evidence. And so, critics insist, fundamentalists are set on a path to believe in "truths" that clearly are not true.

Then, critics say, there is the fear factor. With a busybody God constantly peering over their shoulder checking for doubts and other forbidden behaviors, how can fundamentalists ever be truly at ease in the world? Author and journalist Susan Jacoby, an atheist, speaks of "religious fanatics who are so terrified about what is inside them that they cannot imagine behaving decently without a vengeful God to keep them in line."

Fundamentalists see doubt as a sin and a sign of weakness. Nonfundamentalist believers see it as a virtue and a sign of strength.

4
Secular Corruption

According to George Marsden, a fundamentalist is a believer who is "angry about something." Fundamentalists' anger is typically focused on what they see as immoral behaviors in modern secular society. In his radio program, *The Cutting Edge*, fundamentalist pastor David Bay, director of Old Path Ministries, puts it this way: "The moral bankruptcy of our society is well-documented. . . . [W]hen we look at society through the eyes of God, through the Bible, we can easily see why we are facing the unprecedented troubles today." The troubles of which Bay speaks spring from multiple sources. One is the secular state—government that exists separate from religious beliefs and traditions.

The Corrupt Secular State

Fundamentalists blame secular government for all sorts of ills. They blame it for discouraging religion and religious practices in schools. They blame it for encouraging a wide array of sinful practices such as extramarital sex, same-sex marriage, homosexuality, divorce, abortion, prostitution, gambling, drinking alcoholic beverages, assisted suicide, granting equal rights to gay people, the teaching of evolution in schools, stem cell research, advances in women's rights, and actions to curb and control global warming. Fundamentalists want these secular practices either severely cut back or outlawed. They see the government's failure to do so as a deliberate attack on the traditional religious values they hold dear.

Fundamentalists also see these practices as an attack on what God himself holds dear. On September 11, 2001, radical Muslim terrorists hijacked four U.S. airliners and crashed three of them into the Pentagon and the twin towers of New York's World Trade Center, killing nearly 3,000 people. Jerry Falwell, fundamentalist pastor of a 22,000-member Baptist church, saw the attacks as God's wrathful judgment on the United States for "throwing God out of the public square, out of the schools. The abortionists have got to bear some burden for this because God will not be mocked."

During a broadcast of *The 700 Club*, a Christian television show, Falwell said: "I really believe that the pagans, and the abortionists, and the feminists, and the gays and the lesbians who are actively trying to make that an alternative lifestyle, the ACLU [American Civil Liberties Union], People For the American Way, all of them who have tried to secularize America. I point the finger in their face and say 'you helped this happen.'" The ACLU and People for the American Way are national organizations dedicated to protecting human rights. Falwell later apologized for including gay people and lesbians in his list of people he held partially responsible for the attacks.

In a prayer delivered later during the same show, *700 Club* host Pat Robertson voiced his own views about the secular U.S. government: "We have sinned against Almighty God, at the highest level of our government, we've stuck our finger in your eye. The Supreme Court has insulted you over and over again, Lord. They've taken

SEPTEMBER 2, 1985 $1.95

TIME

Thunder on the Right
The Growth of Fundamentalism

DUSTUP IN MOSCOW
Sparring over Spies and ASATS

The Reverend
Jerry Falwell

THE REVEREND JERRY FALWELL STARTED THE THOMAS ROAD BAP-
TIST CHURCH IN LYNCHBURG, VIRGINIA, IN 1956. BY THE TIME OF
HIS DEATH IN 2007, MEMBERSHIP IN FALWELL'S FUNDAMENTALIST
MEGACHURCH HAD GROWN FROM 35 TO MORE THAN 24,000.

your Bible away from the schools. They've forbidden little children to pray. . . . [O]rganizations have come into court to take the knowledge of God out of the public square of America."

Critics of fundamentalism disagree. They point out that federal and state governments are forbidden from promoting any one religion's worldview. In fact, the First Amendment to the Constitution makes it clear that "Congress shall make no law respecting an establishment of religion."

That's why Robertson is mistaken when he declares that the U.S. Supreme Court has "forbidden little children to pray" in public schools. U.S. public school students have always been free to pray in school voluntarily. But public schools may not order them to pray. That would move schools in the direction of religious indoctrination, of establishing a state religion. Critics have the same reaction to fundamentalists' complaints about homosexuality, abortion, and other legal behaviors that fundamentalists see as immoral. The Constitution forbids the government from promoting the moral standards of any faith, fundamentalist or otherwise.

Corrupt Mainstream Religion

Mainstream churches pose another kind of threat. According to Professors Martin Marty and R. Scott Appleby, fundamentalists believe that these churches are part of a conspiracy to push them and their religion to "the margins of society." Mainstream churches do this by criticizing fundamentalist churches on the one hand and spreading a corrupt, modernized version of faith on the other, fundamentalists say.

Fundamentalists are especially critical of mainstream evangelical churches. The root of *evangelical* is *evangel*, or the "good news" of salvation through Christ. Evangelicals are conservative, born-again Protestants who believe that the Bible is God's truth and feel the need to share with others their faith in Jesus Christ.

Of the estimated 100 million born-again evangelicals in the United States, about half are mainstream believers. The rest are fundamentalists, who are highly critical of mainstream evangelical churches—especially the megachurches, where two thousand or more worshippers typically attend a weekly service.

How do evangelical megachurches attract such large congregations? By making their churches pleasant and entertaining places in which to worship. Instead of traditional Christian hymns sung simply, they sometimes use nontraditional music performed by Christian rock bands. When it does come time to sing a traditional hymn, instead of looking down at hymnals with the lyrics printed out, the congregation may look up and sing along with the words projected on giant screens, karaoke style. Traditional religious symbols such as Jesus on the cross appear rarely, if at all, in megachurches. Instead of hard wooden pews, the seats are padded for comfort. The messages preached tend to be upbeat and optimistic. Members hear little of the criticism of modernism and sinful behavior that members of fundamentalist churches hear from their preachers. These factors add up to a modernized version of the word of God that, with its growing popularity, fundamentalists see as a threat to their traditional brand of religion.

Besides evangelical megachurches, fundamentalists also disapprove of liberal Christian churches that welcome unrepentant sinners such as adulterers or gay men and women. Fundamentalist pastor Bay insists that by accepting sinners, these churches "have denied that man is inherently sinful. Sin itself is denied." He adds that "They have [also] denied the existence of Absolute Truth, substituting the lie that Truth is relative. . . . They have denied that Heaven and Hell are real places, that there is such a thing as Judgment for sin." Bay accuses liberal churches of being "invaded with Satanic falsity masquerading as Truth."

To fundamentalists there is only one true faith, their own. All others are false faiths. The Church of Jesus Christ of Latter-day Saints—the Mormon church—comes in for particular criticism. The Southern Baptist Convention has labeled the Mormon religion a cult, a dangerous false religion.

Television evangelist Pat Robertson's ministry adds its disapproval. That Web site declares: "Mormonism teaches that God is not the only deity and that we all have the potential of becoming gods." When it comes to matters of the spirit, the site says, "the Mormons are far from the truth." Robertson has denounced other mainstream believers, including Hindus, Jehovah's Witnesses, Christian Scientists, and Muslims.

Each of the world's many faiths has its own set of truths, liberal Christians point out. With so many competing faiths offering conflicting versions of God's word, how can we know for certain which is the one true religion? The answer is that there is no such thing. Bruce Bawer writes, each faith presents a different way of understanding "that Jesus taught us to be less concerned with theological particulars than with our love for God and humanity, and that people from diverse traditions can learn from one another about the nature of God."

Some critics see Christian fundamentalism as hopelessly negative and intolerant. Protestant minister Edward Frost describes it as "legalistic, bound to rules that must be obeyed," which he calls "thou shalt nots." And so, Frost laments, fundamentalism has lost the essence of Christianity. "What is lost is an understanding of the truly essential Christian message as having to do with the primacy of love, with reverence for reason and freedom of thought and with compassion, toleration and justice."

5
The Saved and the Unsaved

Fundamentalists tend to see themselves as a persecuted minority whose way of life is under relentless attack by the forces of secular humanism. Conservative politician Newt Gingrich's words from a 2007 speech echo these feelings: "Basic fairness demands that religious beliefs deserve a chance to be heard. It is wrong to single out those who believe in God for discrimination. Yet, today, it is impossible to miss the discrimination against religious believers."

The National Alliance Against Christian Discrimination (NAACD) agrees. The NAACD is a nationwide organization dedicated to exposing and speaking out against what it calls "anti-Christian bias, bigotry, intolerance, defamation, and discrimination towards Bible believers."

Beware of Secondhand Sin

With so much opposition coming at them from mainstream churches and the secular state, how do fundamentalists defend themselves and their religion? One of their strategies is to separate themselves from the corrupt secular world. In this way believers will be less likely to give in to the temptations of secular society. But with God's word and their church leaders to guide them, why are fundamentalists so concerned about giving in to sin?

Even good people steadfastly dedicated to avoiding sin cannot escape the sins of others, writes fundamentalist scholar Harold Brown. "Much has been made of the dangers of secondhand cigarette smoke; there is even greater danger from what we might call secondhand sin." Brown explains, "A careful driver can be killed in an accident caused by a drunk. A chaste adult can contract AIDS from a blood transfusion. In such cases, although the immediate victim did not sin, someone else's abuse of freedom set the deadly chain of events in motion."

For fundamentalists, the problem of secondhand sin goes all the way back to the first two people on Earth, Adam and Eve, who disobeyed God by giving in to sin, as described in Genesis, the first book of the Old Testament. Before their sin, Adam and Eve lived in a peaceful paradise that would satisfy their every need forever. There was no such thing as death in the Garden of Eden; Adam and Eve were immortal. But after they gave in to Satan and sinning, God condemned them, along with the rest of humankind forever, to the burdens of mortality and a weak and sinful nature. "Because of Adam's sin, and all the other sins of history," Brown writes, "the human body and psyche are vulnerable. We cannot always avoid the consequences of evil."

Build an Alternative Culture

Fundamentalists have more than themselves to protect. They must also watch out for the principles and traditions of their religion. To safeguard both their souls and their faith, fundamentalists and other conservative Christians have worked on building an alternative culture separate from secular society. This Christian culture consists of evangelical and fundamentalist churches; Christian day care centers, grade schools, high schools and universities; and Christian books, movies, television stations, music, and Internet sites. There are an estimated 2,000 Christian radio stations and 250 television stations in the United States. A quick Internet search using the word *Christian*, along with any of these Christian culture components, shows how successful fundamentalists and other conservative Christians have been at creating an alternative culture.

This is not to say that fundamentalists and other conservative Christians live their home lives and work at jobs separate from the secular world. Fundamentalists live on the same streets and work at the same jobs as the rest of the population. But they take care to control their exposure to secular culture.

The task of protecting children from the secular world is especially vital, and public schools present a particularly daunting obstacle. Fundamentalist preacher and best-selling author Tim LaHaye writes:

> **Who can deny that [the] basic doctrines of "scientific humanism" or "atheistic humanism" currently dominate public education in America? This, more than any other factor, has relentlessly changed our "Christian consensus" into a "secular consensus," producing the moral meltdown that is rapidly destroying our people and our nation's freedoms, integrity, happiness, and even safety.**

To protect them from this moral meltdown, many fundamentalist parents educate their children themselves, at home. As of 2007, an estimated 2 to 3 percent of U.S.

SOME FUNDAMENTALIST FAMILIES HOMESCHOOL THEIR CHILDREN TO MAKE SURE THEY GET A BIBLICAL EDUCATION.

children were being homeschooled. Jenefer Igarashi has coedited a magazine for Christian homeschooling families. She summed up her attitude toward proper biblically based education this way: "If my child becomes a doctor and saves 1,000 peoples' lives . . . yet does not know God and fails to make it to heaven, all of my teaching was in vain. . . . I will teach him—foremost—REAL life lessons, and that 'The fear of the Lord is the beginning of knowledge.'"

Homeschooled young people can safely complete their education at a fundamentalist Christian college, such as Bob Jones University (BJU) in Greenville, South Carolina.

The Christian Compass

Jenefer Igarashi is a homeschooling parent who teaches her children that the Bible is a guidebook for Christian living. Here's how she used a lesson about Christopher Columbus's journey across the Atlantic Ocean in 1492 to demonstrate how the Bible can guide a person through life.

First, Igarashi and the children discussed how early explorers used maps, compasses, and constellations to guide them. But, Igarashi said, Columbus did not have a map. "Can you even imagine that?" she asked. "How incredibly difficult! What faith he must have had! How could he have done it?"

She talked of how some people can get lost in strange places and even die, walking endlessly but getting nowhere. To emphasize the point, she took the children outside and had them draw a straight line on the sidewalk with chalk and try to walk along it blindfolded. Could they stay along this straight line? They could not, not without someone to guide them.

Back inside, Jenefer read the words of Jesus from the Bible. "I am the light of the world. Whoever follows me will never walk in darkness, but will have the light of life." She finished the lesson by telling the children, "The Bible is how He speaks and leads us. As Christians, it is our compass."

The BJU Web site pledges that students will continue their biblically-based education: "Whatever field of study our students choose, they are taught the importance of having Christ at the center of their lives. Biblical values are integrated in every classroom and every other part of the educational process."

And parents may rest assured that the contagious ills of the secular world will not spread to the BJU campus: "Dishonesty, lewdness, sensual behavior, adultery, homosexuality, sexual perversion of any kind, pornography, illegal use of drugs, and drunkenness are all clearly condemned by God's Word and prohibited here. Further, we believe that biblical principles preclude gambling, dancing, and the beverage use of alcohol."

Follow the Rules

To safeguard their souls and their religious principles, fundamentalists must live by those principles. They must obey the church's strict moral code, rules that set strict standards of conduct for everyday life, based on biblical principles and interpreted by the church's leaders.

This moral code tells believers, in no uncertain terms, which behaviors are acceptable and which are not. Emmanuel Sivan, professor of history at Hebrew University in Jerusalem, Israel, writes that fundamentalist Protestant churches typically ban the same sorts of behaviors that are prohibited at BJU. The rules also stress "strong parental authority over children," Sivan writes, "attendance at prayer and certain other church activities," and "censorship of reading, listening, and viewing material."

As for sexual activity, some fundamentalist churches stress that it should be engaged in by married, heterosexual couples only, and then solely for the purpose of procreation, and that married couples should not engage in sex purely for pleasure. Not all fundamentalists see sexual pleasure as sinful, though. Marriage manuals aimed at fundamentalists urge readers to enjoy the pleasure of sex with their spouses.

As for gay men and women who wish to follow the dictates of fundamentalism, they face a difficult dilemma. They must make what author and gay activist Andrew Sullivan calls "behavioral sacrifices." For example, "a gay man comfortable with his sexual orientation cannot belong to a fundamentalist faith." However, "a gay man who decides to sublimate his entire sexual being into the maintenance of a rigid religious orthodoxy is often an ideal fundamentalist." A gay man willing to sacrifice his true sexual desires in order to be accepted into the faith is often extraordinarily committed to his religion, Sullivan writes, because he has made such an extreme sacrifice in order to remain faithful to it.

Obey Natural Laws

Following strict rules and making behavioral sacrifices is challenging, but the rewards can be gratifying, even liberating. Sullivan writes:

> [F]rom the point of view of the fundamentalist, this experience, far from being suffocating or encumbering, is a form of complete liberation. . . . We have a fundamental choice, the fundamentalist says. We can live in a constant state of doubt . . . or we can embrace a total explanation that liberates the human person from the ordeal of flawed consciousness into the joy of salvation and stable happiness.

According to fundamentalists, this way of life is liberating for a very good reason: It is a natural way of living. All humans have a nature that is given to them by God.

Personal morality and conscience do not enter into the picture. Each person has the identical choice: to embrace this God-given nature or to turn against it.

Christians who think this way are theocentric. They believe that God, not man, is the central aspect of their existence, and that they should behave in ways that God wishes them to behave. Most serious Christians, including fundamentalists, are theocentric. Randall Terry, founder of Operation Rescue, a fundamentalist antiabortion movement, explains: "That means you view the world in His [God's] terms. Theocentrists don't believe man can create law. Man can only embrace or reject law."

Critics take issue with the philosophy of natural law as practiced by fundamentalists, who are carrying things too far. For example, critics do not see how limiting sex to married heterosexual couples and only for purposes of procreation can be called "natural." Instead, it amounts to criminalizing God-given pleasure. This philosophy decrees "not only that one form of sexual activity is preferable to others, but that all others are immoral, disintegrate the human person, and violate God's law," writes Sullivan. He calls this decree "rigid and contrived," "divorced from nature," and "aggressively controlling of human freedom."

Instead of obedience to strict doctrine, liberal Christians say, they believe in diversity of thought and opinion. They welcome discussion on issues of faith because they know they can never have all the answers. Truth is a temporary matter, in constant need of testing by further experience, they insist. From this perspective, fundamentalist demand for strict obedience to unchanging rules is close-minded and wrongheaded.

And liberal Christians do not see the modern secular world as polluting and contagious. The notion of getting "infected" by the sins of others simply from living in the secular world is irrational, alarmist, and above all irresponsible. People must not blame their bad behavior on a supernatural being who is out to get them. They must hold themselves, not Satan, responsible for their thoughts and actions.

Harvest Souls

Besides arming themselves against the corrupting influences of the secular world, fundamentalists must save souls. They must step out into the corrupt world and proselytize. They must "bear witness" by sharing their religion with nonbelievers. They must take part in a "soul harvest," the recruiting of new members. Every soul harvested means another person saved from damnation and another soul added to the faith community.

Where are these souls to be found? Almost anywhere. Some fundamentalist ministries, for example, reach out to prisoners confined to jail cells. Pastor Britt Williams writes: "It is a joy beyond human expression to see men who once lived shattered and useless lives find new hope in Jesus."

And how does one become saved? By faith. A fundamentalist Baptist Web site puts it this way: "If you will receive Jesus Christ as your personal Saviour, believing with all your heart that God has raised Him from the dead, you can be sure that you are saved."

When they talk of being saved, fundamentalists often cite the words of Jesus from the New Testament, John 14:6. Speaking to Thomas, his disciple, Jesus says "I am the way, and the truth, and the life; no one comes to the Father but through Me" (*New American Standard*). There is only one way to live correctly and to attain eternal life, fundamentalists insist, and it is their sacred duty to encourage others to accept this way of life and be saved.

Nonfundamentalist Christians disagree. Fundamentalism holds that "God loves only the 'saved' and that they

HIGHWAY BILLBOARDS ARE ONE WAY FOR FUNDAMENTALISTS AND OTHER CONSERVATIVE CHRISTIANS TO REACH OUT TO NONBELIEVERS AND SAVE SOULS.

alone are truly his children," Bawer writes. But nonfundamentalist Christianity holds that "God loves all human beings and that all are his children."

Liberal Christians tend to see fundamentalism as well-meaning, but also intolerant and misguided. Imagine a mountain with many paths, all leading to the top, they say. All great religions encourage people to lead ethical, positive lives. Therefore all faiths should be respected. No, critics insist, fundamentalists do not have all the answers; they only think they do.

6

Church and State

Christian fundamentalists pledge to do more than avoid the contagious ills of secular society. They insist that they must work to give secular society a makeover by merging religion and politics. They will not be satisfied, they say, until the United States has been returned to the Christian traditions and principles upon which the nation was founded.

Return to Our Christian Roots

In the First Amendment to the U.S. Constitution, these words appear: "Congress shall make no law respecting an establishment of religion, or prohibiting the free exercise thereof." This part of the amendment is known as the Establishment Clause since, as generally interpreted, it establishes a separation between church and state. The state must stay out of the church's business—all churches, all religions—and the church must stay out of the state's business. Religion and law must stay separate.

Fundamentalists disagree with this interpretation of

PRESIDENTIAL CANDIDATE JOHN MCCAIN CONDUCTS A TOWN HALL MEETING IN A NEW HAMPSHIRE CHURCH WHILE LOCAL CHILDREN LISTEN. MCCAIN AGREES WITH CONSERVATIVE CHRISTIANS THAT THE UNITED STATES IS A NATION FOUNDED ON CHRISTIAN PRINCIPLES.

the Establishment Clause. The United States is a Christian nation, they insist, founded on God's word. Among the politicians who agree with them is John McCain, U.S. senator from Arizona. In a 2006 magazine interview, Senator McCain was told of a recent poll determining that 55 percent of Americans believed that the U.S. Constitution established a Christian nation. And what did he think?

"I would probably have to say yes," he answered. "But I say that in the broadest sense. The lady that holds her lamp beside the golden door [the Statue of Liberty] doesn't say, 'I only welcome Christians.' We welcome the poor, the tired, the huddled masses. But when they come here they know that they are in a nation founded on Christian principles."

Fundamentalists believe that for many years the United States has been slipping away from those Christian principles and needs to return to the pure Christian faith of its founders. In a 2007 magazine piece, fundamentalist minister Tim LaHaye wrote that "America's founding was based more on biblical principles than any other nation's on Earth—and that's the main reason this country has been more blessed by God than any other nation in history."

Reverend Pat Robertson was even more direct and insistent. In a 1993 speech, this is what he had to say about church-state separation in the United States: "There is no such thing in the Constitution. It's a lie of the [L]eft, and we're not going to take it anymore."

By "the Left," Robertson meant the liberal-minded politicians and journalists who tend to be critics of Christian fundamentalism. What do these critics think of the notion that the United States was founded on Christian principles?

They point to the two most important founding documents, the Declaration of Independence and the Constitution. The Declaration of Independence does refer to "the

Laws of Nature and of Nature's God." But the Declaration of Independence is not a legislative document. It does not explain how laws shall be made and enforced. The U.S. Constitution does that. And the Constitution is a secular document. It does not mention God or Christianity at all, and religion is mentioned in only two spots. One is the Establishment Clause, where the purpose is to keep church and state lawfully separated from one another. The other spot, which is in Article VI, declares that "no religious test shall ever be required as a qualification to an office or public trust under the United States."

Perhaps the most direct answer to whether the United States was founded as a Christian nation can be found in the *Treaty of Tripoli*, signed in 1797 by John Adams, second president of the United States, which declares that "the Government of the United States of America is not, in any sense, founded on the Christian religion."

The Founding Fathers were not out to establish Christianity as the state religion. On the contrary, they were determined to make certain that the government could never establish any sort of state religion at all. They knew well what had happened in Europe when both Catholics and Protestants agreed that only a single religion must exist in society because there could be only one true religion, and that it was the duty of the state to impose that religion on everyone alike.

The result was the religious intolerance and persecution that had sent the first settlers fleeing from Europe to the North American colonies, where they could worship God in whatever way they believed to be right. Author and essayist Mark Lilla writes that for these early settlers, "establishing a constitutional framework guaranteeing toleration and church-state separation was the first order of political business. Nothing goes deeper in American collective consciousness."

And that church-state separation was successfully

In 2004 the **U.S. Supreme Court** ruled that allowing teachers to lead public schoolchildren in the version of the **Pledge of Allegiance** that contains the words "under God" does not violate the separation of church and state. Here, supporters of the use of "under God" gather outside the **U.S. Supreme Court** as the case is being argued inside.

brought about in the U.S. Constitution. The result is an enduring secular society where anyone may have deep religious convictions of any kind, but where laws are neutral regarding any particular religion. In short, critics of fundamentalism declare, the United States of America was founded as a secular—not a Christian—nation.

Remake the Laws

Fundamentalists are not content to simply keep a distance between themselves and modern secular society. They want to remake the modern world to bring it in line with their strict conservative worldview. The law is a crucial component in this makeover. Fundamentalists want the nation's laws to be biblically based, not secularly based. During the 1970s a series of political movements and organizations supporting this goal came together into a force known as the Christian Right, or the Religious Right. Christian fundamentalists are a vital part of that force, sharing conservative positions on issues such as abortion rights, gay rights, and the teaching of evolution in schools.

The Christian right was an influential voting block within the U.S. Republican Party that helped elect George W. Bush president in 2000 and 2004. In 2000, for example, the Christian Right cast an estimated 15 million votes. According to Bush, Protestant evangelist Billy Graham was responsible for his becoming a born-again Christian after the two had an inspirational talk in 1985. The president's conservative political and social agenda reflected many of the Christian Right's positions on reforming secular society, including the nations' laws.

To say that laws can be neutral of religious values is simply impossible, fundamentalists insist. Any law reflects someone's moral values. They point to *Roe* v. *Wade*, the 1973 U.S. Supreme Court decision that invalidated most laws prohibiting abortion because they violate women's right to privacy. *Roe* sends a strong message that abortion is morally permissible, fundamentalists say, while they believe it to be murder. The Christian Right is dedicated to seeing *Roe* overturned and the practice of abortion outlawed in all fifty states. The same goes for laws that permit pornography, birth control, homosexuality, and other behaviors that they insist violate traditional Christian morals.

Besides electing officials who reflect their moral values, fundamentalists have another strategy for remaking the nation's laws. The key is Christian law schools. Fundamentalist preacher Pat Robertson founded Regent University, in Virginia Beach, Virginia, for that very reason. During President Bush's two terms in office, his administration hired about 150 Regent law school graduates. Regent is among a growing number of conservative Christian law schools that include Liberty University School of Law in Lynchburg, Virginia, founded by fundamentalist preacher Jerry Falwell. Falwell spoke of the need for "a generation of Christian attorneys who could . . . infiltrate the legal profession with a strong commitment to the Judeo-Christian ethic."

Liberty graduated its first law school class in 2007. Matthew Krause was one of those graduates. In a newspaper interview, Krause summed up the Christian right's two-pronged strategy for remaking the nation's legal system: "We don't want abortion, but what are we doing about it? Let's get into the courts and find a way to combat that. Same-sex marriage we don't feel is right or a good thing for the culture. How are we going to stop that? You have to do that through the legal processes. Then, at the same time, vote for politicians who share those ideas and beliefs."

The Abortion Debate

Critics see the fundamentalists as attempting to undermine the U.S. Constitution by demanding that all parts of public life—political, legal, religious, and cultural—conform to their strict moral code. Liberal-minded people of all sorts, including both believers and nonbelievers, agree with Thomas Jefferson, who wrote of "building a wall of separation between Church and State."

What happens if fundamentalists succeed in tearing down that wall? The Christian fundamentalist moral code is only one of many such codes, critics point out. The United States is a nation of different people with differing ideas of what is morally right and wrong. The constitutional wall of separation helps to keep people from stubbornly taking and holding opposing sides on the most basic moral issues. Andrew Sullivan writes, "If you rest your political system on theology . . . you do not solve your problem of establishing a common ground for a political order. You make it much, much worse. You sow the deepest division and the starkest polarization."

A look at the issue of abortion shows how polarization springs up when politics meets religion. Conservative writer and editor William Kristol takes the fundamentalist side on abortion. "The truth is that abortion is today the bloody crossroads of American politics," he writes. Kristol calls the lawful practice of abortion "the focal point for liberalism's simultaneous assault on self-government, morals and nature."

Gary Wills, an influential historian and author, holds an opposing view. Wills, a liberal Christian, writes that fundamentalists take the position dictated by the biblical commandment "Thou shalt not kill." "Fair enough," Wills writes. "But is abortion murder? Most people think not."

As for religion and abortion, Wills writes that it is not treated anywhere in the Old Testament or New Testament. Abortion "is not a theological matter at all. There is no theological basis for either defending or condemning abortion." Abortion is a matter to be decided by reason, not scripture, Wills insists.

Critics point to the abortion debate as a prime example of the confusion that can result when deeply held religious beliefs become part of a debate on secular legal matters. When it comes to religion and politics, critics say, the law should remain as indifferent as possible to the claims made by true believers on behalf of their religion.

The Global Climate Change Debate

Leading climate scientists from nations worldwide agree that human activity is causing the Earth's climate to change in potentially dangerous, even catastrophic ways. Vast amounts of carbon dioxide (CO_2) expelled from automobile exhausts, coal-burning factories' smokestacks, and other humanmade sources of air pollution are causing the ice caps at the North and South Poles to melt. If this melting continues, sea levels worldwide could rise so high that islands and coastlines will begin to disappear. Warming may also be making weather more extreme, increasing incidents of droughts, floods, and hurricanes worldwide. To reduce global warming, experts say, we must pass new laws that help turn us away from gasoline, coal, and other polluting fossil fuels to earth-friendly energy sources such as solar, wind, water, and biomass.

Christian fundamentalists tend to see concern over global warming as another assault by secular liberals on traditional religious values. Fundamentalist preacher Jerry Falwell said, "I can tell you, our grandchildren will laugh at those who predicted global warming. We'll be in global cooling by then, if the Lord hasn't returned. I don't believe a moment of it. The whole thing is created to destroy America's free enterprise system and our economic stability."

As for converting from fossil fuels to Earth-friendly energy, fundamentalists see no need. Why attempt to control the planet's future when we have no say in it? The Creator has already determined the future. Global climate change is God's signal to us that we are living in the End Times, when the son of God will return, true believers will enter heaven, sinners will be sent to hell, and history will end. Until then, the Lord will provide.

Not all conservative Christians agree with fundamentalist thinking on global climate change. The National Association of Evangelicals (NAE), with an estimated 30 million members, is a prominent part of the Christian Right. Its leaders often speak out on behalf of the organization on moral and political issues, such as the NAE's strong opposition to abortion. And some NAE members oppose taking action against global warming.

But others agree with climate experts that this issue demands their attention. In 2007, NAE leaders joined a group of scientists in signing a statement which asked that Americans make serious changes to their lifestyles and laws to avoid disastrous changes in the Earth's climate. NAE official Rich Cizik said, "Science can be an ally in helping us understand what faith is telling us. We will not allow the Creation to be degraded, destroyed by human folly."

Some conservative Christians tend to oppose scientists rather than cooperate with them, since many scientific findings contradict biblically based truths. But this time, said Cizik, "We discovered that we were both speaking from our hearts and our minds. We found we really like each other."

The Evolution Debate

The Bible has nothing to say about abortion or human-made global climate change, but it has lots to say about how life on earth got started. The Book of Genesis states that God made everything—the seas and the land, the plants and the animals, including the first man and the first woman—in six twenty-four-hour days. There were never any primitive life forms from which advanced life forms evolved. Everything appeared abruptly on Earth just as it is today. From their reading of the Bible, Christian fundamentalists declare that a supernatural God ac-

Creation Museum

In Petersburg, Kentucky, natural history is biblical history. At the Creation Museum, exhibits show dinosaurs existing in the same time and space as Adam and Eve, Earth's first human beings, who appeared some six thousand years ago. Placing people and dinosaurs in the same scene defies all the scientific evidence that dinosaurs died out many millions of years before the first ancestors of humans appeared.

Exhibits in the museum's 60,000 square foot space make claim after claim that defy science. For example, that the entire one million–plus acres of the Grand Canyon were carved out in a few hours, and that coal can be formed in the earth in just a few weeks, as opposed to the millions of years scientists say it takes. And the fossils on exhibit are said to be only a few thousand years old, from the time of Noah's flood, when God decided to wipe out all life on the corrupt Earth except for the animals Noah and his family had gathered into the ark.

The events depicted in the history museum's exhibits must be taken on faith. They come entirely from a literal reading of Genesis, which fundamentalists claim is historically and scientifically accurate. "If the Bible is the word of God, and its history really is true, that's our presupposition or axiom, and we are starting there," said the museum's founder, Ken Ham, an evangelist and former high school science teacher. The purpose of the museum, he says, is to counter the scientific point of view with the biblical point of view—the correct point of view.

complished all this some six thousand to ten thousand years ago.

Scientists disagree. In a book about evolution, prominent biologist Edward O. Wilson writes, "[B]iologists are unanimous in concluding that evolution is a fact." They accept Charles Darwin's theory of evolution, which states that life on Earth has been evolving to its present state over many millions of years, and continues to evolve. God plays no part in Darwin's theory. Instead, life has evolved gradually and all on its own, without any assistance from a supernatural Creator.

Fundamentalists offer two different versions of how life on Earth came to be. One is "creationism" or "creation science," the biblically based doctrine that each species of organism was created separately in essentially the same form as it exists today by God in a period of six twenty-four-hour days some six thousand to ten thousand years ago. The other is "intelligent design," the doctrine that life on Earth has evolved gradually over tens of millions of years, much as described in Darwin's theory of evolution, but that this evolution has been guided by a supernatural force of some kind.

Both versions contradict scientific thinking by putting a supernatural Creator into the picture. Presently, U.S. public schools teach only evolution, which does not involve a Creator. Since the U.S. government supports public schools with taxpayer money, public schools must obey federal laws. Fundamentalists have been battling to get new laws passed that would require public schools to teach creationism and intelligent design as alternatives to evolution.

So far they have not succeeded. Their key loss came in the 1987 U.S. Supreme Court ruling in *Edwards* v. *Aguillard*. The Court struck down a Louisiana law that had ordered schools to teach creationism along with evolution.

The Louisiana law was ruled unconstitutional because its purpose was to advance the viewpoint that a supernatural being created humankind. And since this viewpoint was part of the doctrine of certain religious denominations, it violated the Establishment Clause of the First Amendment, which establishes a separation of church and state.

Fundamentalists continue the battle today. They point to national polls indicating that a substantial majority of the American public is on their side. For example, a June 2007 Gallup Poll shows that 66 percent of Americans believe that "God created human beings pretty much in their present form at one time within the last 10,000 years." Why, fundamentalists ask, should a clear majority of Americans pay for public schools that teach only evolution, the opposite of what they believe? Secular society needs to change, fundamentalists insist, to reflect the religious values of its citizens.

The rise in fundamentalism within the United States makes it clear that the belief in God as the Supreme Being and Creator is far from dead. As author and history professor Joel Carpenter says, "Religion is very much alive and very much a factor, not just in people's personal lives but in public affairs."

How big a factor? That remains to be seen. But clearly the battle to remake secular society will continue. And not just in the United States. Fundamentalist movements are growing all around the world, and nowhere with such force and power as in the Arab world.

7
Islamic Fundamentalism

Osama bin Laden is widely assumed to be the mastermind behind the September 11, 2001, attacks against the United States in which nearly three thousand people were killed. Bin Laden is the Saudi leader of al-Qaeda, the radical Islamist group that is also believed to be behind the 1998 terrorist bombings of American embassies in the East African nations of Kenya and Tanzania.

Bin Laden's stated reasons for attacking the United States show clear similarities between his point of view and that of Christian fundamentalists. In his "Letter to the American People," issued on the Internet in November 2002, bin Laden gave those reasons:

> You are the nation who . . . choose to invent your own laws as you will and desire. You separate religion from your policies, contradicting the pure nature which affirms Absolute Authority to the Lord and your Creator. You flee from the embarrassing

OSAMA BIN LADEN HAS REPEATEDLY CONDEMNED THE UNITED
STATES FOR INTERFERING WITH POLITICAL AFFAIRS IN THE ARAB
WORLD. PAKISTANI ISLAMISTS CARRY BIN LADEN'S PHOTO DURING
THIS 2002 PROTEST AGAINST U.S. MILITARY ACTIVITIES.

question posed to you: How is it possible for Allah the Almighty to create His creation, grant them power over all the creatures and land, grant them all the amenities of life, and then deny them that which they are most in need of: knowledge of the laws which govern their lives?

According to bin Laden, the attacks of September 11, 2001, were all America's fault. Like all the world's people, Americans owe their very existence to God, Allah, the creator and ruler of the entire Earth. Allah has been wonderfully generous to humankind. In addition to bestowing the gift of life, Allah has made human beings the most powerful of all the planet's life forms. And how have Americans responded to Allah's gifts? By creating a secular society based on their own laws separate from Allah's laws. Has not Allah, in the scriptures, given Americans the laws he expects them to follow as they enjoy the precious life he has so graciously bestowed upon them? And yet Americans arrogantly deny Allah's laws. And for that arrogance Allah has righteously punished them.

Osama bin Laden belongs to a fundamentalist group within the Sunni sect of Islam which speaks of *ghatrasa*, or the arrogance of replacing God's laws with secular, humanmade laws. His statement of blame recalls similar statements by Christian fundamentalist preachers Jerry Falwell and Pat Robertson. Falwell warned that "God will not be mocked" and laid the blame for the 9/11 attacks on liberals for "throwing God out of the public square" and trying to "secularize America."

Here we see Falwell and bin Laden, two men on opposite sides in the War on Terror, sharing a deep mutual resentment of U.S. secular society. They agree that liberal Americans have rejected God's laws in favor of their own humanmade laws, and that for that reason they justly deserve God's punishment. Falwell and bin Laden agree because their brand of faith is stronger to them than any national or cultural allegiance. For the fundamentalist, Christian or Islamic, God comes before country, before anything.

A Strict Set of Rules

Only Christianity, with its many different religions, is larger than Islam. More than one billion Muslims live in today's world. The Islamic faith thrives in Africa, Asia, and the Middle East, with large Islamic immigrant populations in Europe, Canada, and the United States. Islam has several sects, or branches. The Sunni sect is by far the largest, with about 940 million members worldwide. Most other Muslims belong to the Shia sect and are known as Shiites.

Each sect claims to be the true branch of Islam, and this rivalry leads to disagreement and tension. But all Islamic sects agree on one thing: Islam is not a Sunday kind of religion. Fundamentalist Muslims do more than gather to worship once or twice a week. Muslims must pray at least five times a day every day. And throughout the day they must practice Muslim virtues such as discipline, humility, sacrifice, patience, self-restraint, generosity, and submission to Allah. *Islam* is an Arabic word that means "peace through submission to the will of Allah." Every moment of a true Muslim's waking life must be lived according to the guidance of Allah.

To rightly practice these virtues, true Muslims must follow a strict set of rules meant to guide their everyday thoughts and actions. These rules are contained in teachings revealed by Allah through the Prophet Muhammad bin Abdullah, a mortal messenger of the immortal Creator, in the seventh century CE. Muhammad (sometimes spelled Mohammed) lived from 570 to 632.

The Quran and Shariah

The Prophet Muhammad's teachings are collected in the Quran, the central religious text of Islam. Along with the Sunnah, it forms the basis of the faith. Other sacred texts include the Hadith, the recorded sayings and deeds of the prophet; and the Sira, traditional biographies of Muhammad.

The Quran's 114 *surahs*, or chapters, are all said to have come down to humankind in a chain starting with Allah himself, who passed them to one of his angels—Gabriel—who then passed them down to the Prophet Muhammad on earth. Muhammad then dictated Allah's revelations to his followers, who faithfully wrote them down. After Muhammad's death, they put them together to form the Quran: the final revealed truth of Allah.

The Sunnah, Hadith, and Sira quote the Prophet and tell about his life, but their words are not said to have come directly from Allah. Fundamentalist Muslims accept the Quran the way fundamentalist Christians accept the Bible, as the true word of the Creator. They do not reinterpret the Quran in terms of modern thinking. They are dedicated to protecting its truths and maintaining them unchanged.

But the Quran is not only a religious text. It is the basis of Islamic law. In a strict Muslim nation such as Iraq or Afghanistan, religion and government are intermingled in a theocracy. Iraq's constitution states, "No law that contradicts the established provisions of Islam may be established." The constitution of Afghanistan declares, "No law can be contrary to the beliefs and provisions of the sacred religion of Islam." Everything—religion, culture, politics—is governed by *Shariah*, the body of Islamic law based on the Quran and other sacred texts. In Shariah, the laws are attributed not to men but to God, as reported by the Prophet Muhammad.

Even in Muslim nations ruled by secular governments, such as Egypt, Algeria, and Indonesia, a mixture of Shariah law and secular law is in effect. In these nations, fundamentalists want to eliminate all secular influence until everyone lives exclusively by the morals and laws revealed in Islamic scripture.

Jihad

But the most radical of Islamic fundamentalists have a more wide-ranging goal in mind, an ultimate mission that extends beyond their nation's geographic borders. They look forward to a time when all nations are purified from non-Islamic practices, when the entire planet consists of a single pan-Islamic state based on Shariah.

This mission is a form of *jihad*, an Arabic word with three distinctly different meanings. The first is a call to inner spiritual struggle, a struggle to overcome forbidden desires that prevent the good Muslim from achieving complete submission to the will of Allah. The second meaning is a call to convert others to Islam by means of the Quran. All true Muslims are expected to answer these calls.

Jihad's third meaning is an urgent call to defend the faith from its enemies by means of the sword. This call to holy war is to be answered only in times of great need, when the faith is threatened by infidels, unbelievers. A person who dies in a holy war can be sure of spending eternity in *Jannah*, Heaven.

Bin Laden is Islam's foremost inspirational leader when it comes to defending the faith by the sword. Bin Laden himself was inspired by Sayyid Qutb (pronounced KUH-tahb), an Egyptian scholar who predicted an all-out struggle between Islam and the West. Qutb wrote: "[T]his struggle is not a temporary phase, but an eternal state, because truth and falsehood cannot coexist on this earth. . . . The eternal struggle for the freedom of man will

ON APRIL 13, 2001, IN A RALLY AT A REFUGEE CAMP IN GAZA, ABOUT FORTY MASKED MEN, SHROUDED IN WHITE SHEETS—A SYMBOL OF MARTYRDOM TO PALESTINIANS—RENEWED THEIR VOWS AS MEMBERS OF THE ISLAMIC JIHAD TO KILL ISRAELIS.

continue until all religion is for Allah and man is free to worship and obey his Sustainer." According to Qutb and his modern-day followers, a worldwide military showdown between Muslims and Westerners is inevitable, and the result will be victory for Islam.

Basic Beliefs

Like their Christian counterparts, Islamic fundamentalists believe in the Creator as the supernatural force of Good, and in Satan, Shaitan, as the supernatural force of Evil. They also believe that the faithful will be rewarded with the glories and pleasures of *Jannah* while unbelievers will be punished in *Jahannam*, Hell. As stated in the believer's prayer from the Quran: "Our Lord, give us good in this life and good in the next, and save us from the punishment of the Fire" (2:201).

Ruqaiyyah Waris Maqsood is a religious scholar and the author of books on Islam. In an interview with the British Broadcasting Company, she was asked to explain a Muslim's relationship with God: "[True Muslim believers] would do anything rather than offend Allah, and they of course believe that Allah sees every single thing that is done—there are no secrets. Even if you get away with something on Earth, it has been seen and recorded and you will have to face judgment for it eventually." And that judgment could be harsh. Like Jesus in the Bible, the Prophet Muhammad in the Quran warned that the world would endure terrible wars and moral corruption until history came to a violent end, as ordained by Allah. The true believers, who had submitted to Allah, would be saved, while the unbelievers would be damned and tormented for eternity.

These beliefs—in the infallible Quran, God and Satan, Heaven and Hell, the End Times, total submission, and absence of doubt—are basic to Muslim believers. Like their Christian counterparts, Islamic fundamentalists must accept their religion's beliefs completely. As the Quran says, "The Truth is from thy Lord; so be not at all in doubt" (2:147). But to Islamic fundamentalists, faith alone is not sufficient. Believers must live by these beliefs day in and day out even if that means engaging in violent jihad. To do anything less is to be less than a true Muslim.

Islamic fundamentalists are the extreme right-wing faction of the faith. They represent only a small percentage

The Making of a Radical Jihadist

Egyptian scholar Sayyid Qutb visited Greeley, Colorado, in 1949. The Egyptian government had sent him there to study the U.S. educational system. Qutb had never spent time in a Western society before, and the behavior he witnessed in Greeley during his six-month stay deeply disturbed him.

"Everywhere there are smiles and everywhere there is fun and on every corner hugs and kisses," he wrote to friends in Egypt. "But never does one see contentment on a person's face. There is no indication of satisfaction in anyone's heart."

Qutb wrote that most Americans did not go to church and that they were more concerned with themselves and one another than with God. One event in particular colored Qutb's thinking. One evening after the service, a dance was held at a local Protestant church. By Western standards the dance was quite modest and tame. But Qutb was a devout conservative Muslim, and by his standards the dance was anything but tame.

"The dance hall convulsed to the tunes on the gramophone [record player] and was full of bounding feet and seductive legs," an outraged Qutb later wrote. "Arms circle waists, lips met lips, chests met chests, and the atmosphere was full of passion."

Qutb had reason to be shocked. By Western standards, Muslim society is quite conservative. By tradition the sexes are kept apart in schools, mosques, and other public places, and women in public are covered head to toe. Unmarried men and women are not supposed to touch one another. Never before had Qutb witnessed such a shocking display of public physical contact between the sexes.

In the years to follow, Qutb would become the most influential Islamic fundamentalist thinker of his time, and the most anti-Western. He would write that Westerners, with their corrupt culture, were satanic infidels, which made them legitimate targets for violent attacks. Qutb would also write vicious critiques of secular governments in Arab nations, including his homeland of Egypt, condemning them for basing their legitimacy on human rather than divine authority. These diatribes would prove to be his undoing. Sayyid Qutb was put to death in 1966. Egyptian leaders in President Gamal Abdel Nasser's secular government felt threatened by Qutb's calls for violent rebellion, and ordered his hanging. But Qutb's writings would live on, fueling radical Islamic terrorism around the world.

of Islamic believers. But their influence is far greater than their number would indicate. To broadcast and publicize their goals, they resort to extreme tactics—violent political demonstrations and acts of terrorism—that attract media attention and inspire widespread fear. These extremist tactics also stir up strife among the various factions of Islam, pushing them toward revolution and civil war.

Moderate Muslims

The majority of Muslims are moderates. They do not side with radical fundamentalist groups. They do not support violent jihad. And while they dare not speak out about it publicly for fear of retribution, the terrorist violence inflicted on innocent people in the name of Allah shocks and disturbs them.

Then there are those in the Arab world who insist on speaking out against the extremist tactics of fundamentalist Islam despite the risk. These liberal-minded Muslims make it known that their society must move further away from the ancient traditions of Shariah and closer to the modern world, and they stage demonstrations in support of this pro-modernist cause.

These moderate and liberal factions are at odds with Islamic fundamentalists on a variety of issues. Next we explore how each faction responds to modernism.

8

Return to Tradition

Islamic fundamentalism is the most antisecular, antimodern form of Islam. It is also the most conservative form. Islamic fundamentalists reject much about the modern, secular, Western world.

Why? Modernization is nothing new, but globalization is. Starting in the late 1990s, people began taking special note of the speed with which the world's nations were reaching out to one another across geographical boundaries. *Globalization* was the name given to this phenomenon. Nations that used to be strangers were establishing more and more links. Computers and the Internet are big reasons why developing nations in Asia, Africa, and the Middle East are trading more and communicating more with the richer, more industrialized nations in the West, and in the process becoming more wealthy, industrialized, and Westernized themselves.

As a result, waves of Western culture, in the form of computer and Internet technology, movies, television programs, music, clothing, and things to eat and drink, keep

ALMOST ONE MILLION PILGRIMS VISIT MECCA, SAUDI ARABIA, FROM
ALL OVER THE WORLD DURING THE MONTH OF RAMADAN. HERE THEY
CELEBRATE THE NIGHT WHEN THE ANGEL GABRIEL FIRST REVEALED THE
WORDS IN THE QURAN TO THE PROPHET MUHAMMAD.

rolling into developing nations. And the people in these nations keep moving from rural areas to big cities in ever-increasing numbers. By 2009, experts say, population history will be made. For the first time, more of the world's people will be living in cities than in the countryside, and the trend will continue indefinitely. In crowded cities, avoiding contact with what Christian fundamentalists call secondhand sin is all but impossible. Temptations to stray from traditional ways are all around.

Islamic fundamentalists see this cultural invasion from the West as a threat to everything that defines them, all they hold dear: their community, their family life, their religion—their entire conservative lifestyle. This threat is especially dangerous to young people. Western-style movies, television programs, and music lure Muslim youth. Images of a blatantly materialistic and sexually liberated lifestyle tempt them to reject the cultural norms and traditions of Islam. Fundamentalists believe that this assault on their way of life can be counteracted only by a return to the strict rituals and rules of Shariah.

Rituals and Rules

A religious ritual is a strict set of actions designed to keep people in close contact with their faith. In Islam, the practice of prayer, *salat*, is the primary daily ritual. Five times each day Muslims pray: at dawn (*al-fajr*), midday (*al-zuhr*), afternoon (*al-'asr*), sunset (*al-maghrib*) and evening (*al-'isha*). Kneeling on a prayer rug, the supplicant—the person praying—faces eastward, toward the Ka'ba shrine in Mecca, Saudi Arabia. Purification of the flesh is especially important in this ritual, to show love and respect for Allah. To prepare for salat, people wash their hands, mouth, nose, face, arms, head, ears, and feet—all three times each. If no water is available, the Quran says, "then take for yourselves clean sand or earth, and rub therewith your faces and hands" (5:6).

The most important yearly ritual is *Ramadan*, the month of fasting. It takes place during the ninth month of the Islamic calendar. The Quran tells why: "Ramadan is the (month) in which was sent down the Quran, as a guide to mankind, also clear (Signs) for guidance and judgment (between right and wrong). So every one of you who is present (at his home) during that month should spend it in fasting." (2:185) For each day of that month, from sunrise to sundown, no food or drink may be consumed. Smoking and sex are also forbidden. The purpose of Ramadan is to develop self-control, devotion to Allah, and sympathy for the poor.

Religion-based rules spell out how believers should behave in everyday life. In fundamentalist Islamic groups, for example, women may not wear jewelry, cosmetics, or Western-style clothing. In fundamentalist Hindu groups, men must leave their hair uncut and keep it wrapped up in a turban. In the fundamentalist Jewish group known as Haredi, men must grow long beards and dress in black coats and hats.

In fundamentalist religion these rules are extensive, covering not only what one wears but what one eats, drinks, reads, watches, and listens to. Other rules regulate dating behavior, sexual behavior, and marriage. All these strict rules, which apply equally to everyone, go directly against the Western notion that individual freedom of choice brings happiness. For the fundamentalist, happiness is synonymous with religious virtue, not freedom. "Is this kind of behavior virtuous?" the fundamentalist asks. "Does religious law allow it?" If not, one avoids it, because true happiness lies inside the boundaries of virtuous behavior only. Outside those boundaries, happiness is not possible.

Interpreting Shariah

Traditionally, Shariah is interpreted and enforced by a select group of Muslim clerics, or clergymen. Muslim clerics are exclusively male. Some clerics act as out-of-court advisers to people who come to them with questions about what is right and what is wrong under Shariah law. Others act as judges, enforcing Shariah rituals and rules by handing down legal decisions in a Shariah court of law. Their rulings, both in-court and out-of-court, are drawn from the Quran and other sacred texts.

Shariah rulings are known as *fatwas*. Fatwas on the same issue will vary from one Muslim society to another. Take the issue of *salat*. According to the Quran, a Muslim must pray five times daily. Normally, exceptions are made for people who are ill or who are traveling. In the late 1990s in Afghanistan, when that nation was under the strict fundamentalist rule of the Taliban, the rule was strictly interpreted, no exceptions allowed.

In Turkey, an Islamic nation with a secular government, things were different. In October 2007, a Muslim scholar issued a fatwa allowing any Turkish Muslim who so desired to pray only three times a day. Some people objected, but others saw the fatwa as a sensible change based on modern conditions. Jamal al-Banna, a prominent Islamic theologian, said, "Merging prayers has become a modern necessity. In most cases, people do not always perform the five prayers on time due to the pressures of modern life."

Fundamentalist Muslims take a harsh view of their more liberal counterparts, especially in nations where Shariah is strictly interpreted, such as Saudi Arabia. In 2007 a Saudi cleric, Sheikh Saleh al-Fozan, went so far as to issue a fatwa against liberal Muslims: "Calling oneself a liberal Muslim is a contradiction in terms . . .

A Cautionary Tale

The potential drawbacks of religion-based rules lie in the motives of the people who enforce them. Within extreme fundamentalist groups, the rules can become the basis for a joyless, oppressive society. This is what happened in 1996 in Afghanistan when a fundamentalist militia of Sunni Muslims known as the Taliban took over the government. *Taliban* (sometimes spelled *Taleban*) means "religious students."

The country had been caught up in a long civil war, and the Afghan people welcomed an end to the fighting. Their relief did not last long. The new rulers turned out to be corrupt warlords with a passion for dealing out punishment. The Taliban used Shariah as an instrument of oppression, adding all sorts of new prohibitions and strictly enforcing them. The Taliban "religious police" would patrol the streets for signs of what they saw as "un-Islamic behavior."

One of the first activities they banned was one of Afghanistan's most popular pastimes, kite flying. It was frivolous, the Taliban decided: silly, pointless. Andrew Sullivan writes, "What the Taliban did not get—what they, in fact, actively opposed—was what free people feel in their bones: the pursuit of seemingly pointless happiness is the point."

The list of "un-Islamic" activities grew and grew: listening to any kind of music, watching any kind of movies or television, using the Internet. Men were prohibited from shaving or trimming their beards. Women could not appear on the balconies of their apartments or houses. And much, much more.

The "religious police" were free to punish violators on the spot. Or they could arrest them and, later, have them punished in public. Harsh punishments—ranging from floggings to executions—were staged for public view in soccer stadiums. The Taliban's oppressive rule ended in 2001, when U.S. troops invaded Afghanistan and deposed them for their role in supporting the terrorists responsible for the September 11, 2001, terrorist attacks on the United States. But by 2007 they were back in power in parts of Afghanistan, despite the continued presence of U.S. armed forces.

nature, and excess is never just." In the eyes of many non-fundamentalist Muslims today, these harsh punishments amount to violations of basic human rights. Speaking of the Saudi rape case, CNN reporter Carol Costello told television viewers, "This is not a woman's tale of woe—it is a human rights issue."

Muslim scholar Ruqaiyyah Waris Maqsood defends this fundamentalist interpretation of Shariah law: "The usual criticisms of Shariah—that it is so cruel as regards execution, flogging and cutting off hands—totally ignore all the extenuating circumstances that would lead to these penalties not being applied," Maqsood writes. People who criticize these punishments do not understand the positive effects they have on Muslim societies. "[T]he cutting off of a hand for theft is a very powerful deterrent," she insists. "Muslims care less for the callous and continual thief than they do for the poor souls who are mugged and robbed and hurt by the thieves. . . . Most thieves would think twice before risking a hand on mugging an old lady for her handbag!"

Islamic fundamentalists want a strict return to Shariah to protect their religious traditions. One of those traditions is the treatment of women.

9

Men and Women

What about gender equality in Islamic society? How "equal" are the sexes? In terms of who is more precious to Allah, the answer lies in surah 4, verse 124 of the Quran: "If any do deeds of righteousness—be they male or female—and have faith, they will enter Paradise, and not the least injustice will be done to them." Allah loves righteous men and righteous women equally, and both are equally welcome in Heaven.

As for life on earth, things are different. Traditional Islamic society is patriarchal. The male is the head of the family, as decreed in surah 4, verse 34 of the Quran:

Men are the protectors and maintainers of women, because Allah has given the one more (strength) than the other, and because they support them from their means. Therefore the righteous women are devoutly obedient, and guard in (the husband's) absence what Allah would have them guard. As to those women on whose part ye

fear disloyalty and ill-conduct, admonish them (first), (next), refuse to share their beds, (and last) beat them (lightly); but if they return to obedience, seek not against them Means (of annoyance): For Allah is Most High, great (above you all).

Allah has created men as the superior sex and expects them to take care of women, the weaker sex. Women are expected to obey men and keep their bodies modestly covered so as not to tempt any men to whom they are not married. Husbands are expected to discipline wives who disobey them and, if necessary, to physically punish them. If women are obedient, men are not to discipline them.

But that is not all that Islam has to say on this matter. In the last sermon he gave before his death, the prophet issued men this decree: "Remember that you have taken them as your wives only under Allah's trust and with His permission. If they abide by your right, then to them belongs the right to be fed and clothed in kindness. Do treat your women well and be kind to them for they are your partners and committed helpers."

Remove Temptation: Dress Codes

In traditional Muslim society, virtue and honor go hand in hand. The man's honor depends upon the woman's virtue, and the woman's virtue depends largely on her sexual conduct. Both women and men are forbidden from having sex with anyone to whom they are not married. Violators, male or female, bring dishonor on the entire extended family, including grandparents, aunts, uncles, and cousins. But the woman is seen as the source of temptation, so strict measures are taken to guard her virtue.

MUSLIM PARENTS AND THEIR CHILDREN LOOK OUT AT THE INDIAN OCEAN IN THE SOUTHERN ASIAN NATION OF SRI LANKA. MUSLIM TRADITION DICTATES THAT ADULT WOMEN REMAIN COVERED FROM HEAD TO TOE, EVEN AT THE BEACH.

A dress code is one measure. A woman in public view presents a potential temptation to men. That is why surah 33, verse 59 of the Quran states: "Tell thy wives and thy daughters and the women of the believers to draw their cloaks close round them (when they go abroad). That will be better, so that they may be recognised and not annoyed." Whenever a woman leaves the home, she must be properly dressed so as not to draw the attention of men.

Fundamentalist Muslims insist that women in public be clothed from head to toe at all times, in loose-fitting garments that disguise her figure. *Hijab*, the Arabic word for this full dress code, means "covered." The code includes rules for what jewelry the woman may wear, how much makeup she is allowed, and how her feet should be covered. Hijab varies from one Muslim society to another. Many women in Afghanistan, India, and Pakistan, for instance, wear a *burqa*, a loose outer garment that envelops the body from head to toe, worn over her other clothing when she is out in public, and removed when she returns home. A woman who dresses according to the standards of hijab is expected to remain safe from the unwelcome attentions of men.

How do Muslim women feel about this dress code? According to religious scholar Ruqaiyyah Waris Maqsood, "Some Muslim women feel that they should cover everything from neck to ankle, and neck to wrist. Others also include a head veil . . . and finally some choose to cover even their faces, although there is no Islamic text requiring this extreme."

Maqsood, who lives in Great Britain, states that "when men try to enforce Muslim dress on women, this is forbidden—no aspect of our faith is to be done by coercion." In some fundamentalist-minded Islamic nations, though, hijab is still enforced. In the kingdom of Saudi Arabia, for example, women are expected to wear an *abaya*, a plain black robe, in public. Until a few years ago, members of the Commission for the Promotion of Virtue and the Prevention of Vice, would patrol the streets of the Saudi seaport, Jiddah, looking for violators. These fundamentalist policemen carried sticks to administer on-the-spot punishments.

But times are slowly changing. In Jiddah, the kingdom's most modern city, the vice police have become a thing of the past, and some young women are challenging the dress code. They can be seen with their head scarves around their shoulders and their abayas left open to show their clothing beneath. In Jiddah's Western-style shopping malls, medical students in colorful head scarves and lab coats over jeans wear no abaya at all. And brightly colored abayas with animal and flower patterns are showing up in shops in Jiddah and other Saudi cities.

Fundamentalist-minded clerics object to these trends. Women in public should always wear abayas, which should never be brightly colored. An abaya is meant to divert the man's attention from the woman, not attract it. Clerics have issued fatwas outlawing all but dark and shapeless abayas, and many Saudi women approve. Manal al-Sharif, a newspaper editor, told a *Washington Post* reporter that she dresses conservatively at all times. "God ordered women to dress modestly, to be respectable and to avoid provoking lust," she declared.

Remove Temptation: Confinement

Confinement is another measure to ensure virtue. In nations where Shariah law is strictly enforced, a woman is not allowed out in public unless accompanied by a male relative, and she may not meet privately with a man to whom she is not related. Other prohibitions include driving an automobile, riding in a taxi without a male relative along, sitting in the same room with men in coffee bars, and voting in elections.

The consequences for violating these male-female restrictions can be harsh. For having sex outside of marriage, one hundred lashes is common. To Westerners these punishments may seem extreme, but many Muslims disagree. Maqsood explains why:

> **In the West, adultery has become so commonplace because of sexual freedoms—all the emphasis these days seems to be on finding sexual satisfaction; in Muslim societies, there is far less emphasis on sex—it is usually regarded as a weakness that can lead to all sorts of trouble. Family is far more important; the notion of a million unborn children per year being aborted, and single mothers, is abhorrent in Islam.**

In other words, when it comes to sexual relations, in the Western world the emphasis is on freedom of choice, even though this sometimes leads to abortions and single-parent families. In the Muslim world the emphasis is on protecting family life. Punishing adultery helps prevent problems that are far more costly in terms of family stability and loss of human life than is the loss of freedom to have sex with someone to whom one is not married.

Remove Temptation: Arranged Marriages

The Creator does not wish believers to remain single. The Quran commands all Muslims to marry. To make sure that a woman marries honorably and well, male relatives may arrange the marriage for her. Often the man they choose is a member of the extended family, a first cousin who is the child of the father's brother or the mother's sister. This means that everyone will know the marriage partners well and so can arrange a suitable match.

Arranged marriages are good for all concerned, fundamentalists insist. They help guard the young woman's

Escape From Kabul

When West meets East, events sometimes take unexpected and unfortunate turns. Phyllis Chesler, an American woman, met her future husband, a native of Afghanistan, at a U.S. college where both were students. They lived a Western lifestyle, with none of the restrictions that Islam puts on a woman. Then they married and moved to Kabul, Afghanistan's capital city, to begin their married life. This was in the 1960s, before the Taliban took over, but Afghanistan was a strict fundamentalist nation even then.

Almost immediately, Chesler wrote, "my husband became a stranger." The man who was her equal in America became her overseer in Kabul. She was treated like the other women in her husband's extended family. "I was supposed to lead a largely indoor life among women, to go out only with a male escort and to spend my days waiting for my husband to return."

Individually, Afghans were friendly and courteous, Chesler wrote, and Afghanistan was a beautiful country. But the treatment of women outraged her Western temperament. The Quran allows a man up to four wives, and her husband's father had three. Women riding buses had to sit in the back. They were not allowed to pray in the mosques. Marriages were arranged. All these customs led to what she called "chronic female suffering."

She managed to get back to the United States and escape her marriage in Afghanistan. Today Chesler is a renowned author of books on women's rights and a professor of psychology and women's studies at the City University of New York.

virtue, since there is no dating that could lead to premarital sex. The woman benefits because she is assured that she will have a spouse, and the parents benefit because the woman remains in their complete care and control until she is married.

Under Shariah law a woman does enjoy the right to refuse an arranged marriage. But family pressures tend to make refusal an act of rebellion that brings dishonor, making it difficult for the woman not to accept the extended family's choice of husband.

Women React to Restrictions

These restrictions on a woman's conduct are designed to stabilize Muslim society. Women's rights are limited, but they can rest assured that they know what is expected of them. When they accept these limitations, life becomes more certain for them, and with certainty comes comfort. But what if a woman is not comfortable living under the restrictions of Shariah law? Then she may protest the situation, individually or as part of a group.

In May 2007, an interview was broadcast on Al Hurra TV with Saudi women's rights activist Wajiha al-Huweidar. Al Hurra television broadcasts in Arabic to the Middle East, but the United States pays for Al Hurra. Al-Huweidar's blunt criticisms would not be welcome on standard Saudi television, in a nation that enforces strict Shariah law. "Saudi society is based on masters and slaves, or, to be more precise, masters and maids," she declared, "because the masters are the men, and slaves are the women. . . . Women today are not allowed to make any kind of decision—not about marriage, work, studies, medical treatment, leaving the house, or traveling."

Why aren't more women protesting Shariah restrictions? "[W]hen a man . . . calls for equality and liberalism, he is highly respected. . . . Even the [government] shows respect for a man who speaks freely, but it shows no respect for a woman who speaks freely. She pays the price on every level—her family, religion, and society." Al-Huweidar has spent time in prison for her outspoken criticism of the treatment of women in her country.

She is not alone. Iran is another fundamentalist Islamic society ruled by a strict theocracy. In March 2007, Iranian security forces arrested more than thirty women's rights activists. Their crime? They were rallying outside a court in the capital city of Tehran, protesting a trial of five women protesters who took part in an earlier demonstration against Shariah laws that the protesters said discriminated against women.

IN BLACKBURN, GREAT BRITAIN, A MUSLIM WOMAN DEMONSTRATES IN FAVOR OF THE VEIL. SHE AND OTHER DEMONSTRATORS ARE REACTING TO A BRITISH POLITICAL LEADER'S COMMENTS AGAINST WEARING VEILS.

Most Muslim women, though, still accept the restrictions of Shariah, even highly educated young women in strict fundamentalist nations. Megan K. Stack, a reporter for the *Los Angeles Times*, observed this fact during a trip to Riyadh, Saudi Arabia, in June 2005. A Saudi politician who was running for office in an upcoming election invited Stack to his home to meet his daughter. The daughter was about the same age as the reporter and spoke fluent English. Stack asked how she felt about not being allowed to vote in the upcoming election. Shariah law in Saudi Arabia allows only men to cast ballots in government elections. The daughter replied that she did not need to vote. "Maybe you don't want to vote," the reporter asked. "But wouldn't you like to make that choice yourself?"

"If I have a father or a husband, why do I need to vote? Why should I need to work?" the daughter answered. "They will take care of everything."

Stack spoke with other women of various ages and backgrounds in Saudi Arabia, and their comments left her with these questions: "Can the country opt to develop in some ways and stay frozen in others? Can the kingdom evolve economically and technologically in a global society without relinquishing its particular culture of extreme religious piety and ancient tribal code?"

That is, can the Kingdom of Saudi Arabia continue to operate under customs and laws whose roots are some 1,300 years old and still be part of a rapidly changing global society? The same question can be asked about Afghanistan, Iran, and other fundamentalist Muslim nations. We now explore this question in terms of fundamentalist Islam's attitudes toward science and education.

10
Science and Education

A thousand years ago the Islamic world was in the midst of its Golden Age. Middle Eastern cities such as Cairo and Baghdad were becoming the world's great storehouses of knowledge for philosophy and science going all the way back to ancient Greece and Rome. Muslim scholars were translating this priceless knowledge into Arabic, which had become the international language of mathematics and science. Arabic and European scholars alike used the facts and ideas in these Arabic translations to help them make revolutionary breakthroughs. For example, the number zero was introduced; the paths of veins and arteries that carry blood throughout the human body were traced; and stars were given names.

What Went Wrong

Islam's Golden Age lasted from the ninth through the thirteenth centuries. Many of Europe's discoveries in science and mathematics in later years owed a debt to the work of Muslim scholars from the Golden Age. In the sixteenth century, for instance, the Polish astronomer Nicolaus Copernicus revealed his revolutionary discovery that the Sun, not the Earth, was the center of the solar system. His discovery is widely believed to be based on the work of Nasir al-Din al-Tusi, a thirteenth century Persian mathematician.

But after the thirteenth century, the development of science and mathematics in the Arab world came to an end. No major inventions or discoveries have come from the Arab world since then. Turkish-American physicist and author Taner Edis says: "Even the most conservative Muslim realizes that the Islamic world is at a severe disadvantage right now in science and technology. The West has done a much better job."

Why? As we have seen, religion based on the supernatural world and science based on the natural world do not work well together. When the discoveries of scientists contradict religious tradition, a tug-of-war debate over who is right springs up. In Europe, religion and science became separated from one another during the periods known as the Renaissance and the Enlightenment, lasting roughly from the fourteenth through the eighteenth centuries. With less in the way of religious opposition, European scientists were freer to investigate the natural world and share their discoveries with the public. This same sort of separation between religion and science failed to take place in the Muslim world. Science continued to take a backseat to religion.

God and Science

The roots of this failure can be found in the Quran. Surah 39, verses 62–63: "Allah is Creator of all things, and He is Guardian over all things. His are the keys of the heavens and the earth." And surah 11, verse 6: "No creature is

THIS SIXTEENTH-CENTURY PAINTING DEPICTS TURKISH ASTRON-
OMERS AT THE GALATA TOWER IN ISTANBUL, TURKEY. DESPITE
THE LOWERING OF THE VEIL ON SCIENCE, SOME MUSLIM SCIENCE
WAS STILL SHOWN.

there crawling on the earth, but its provision rests on God. He knows its lodging place and its repository."

That is, the Creator does not just create living things. He also causes them to remain alive and causes them to die. Allah is the ultimate cause of whatever happens to all living things. The Creator, not nature, is the primary cause of everything. The so-called laws of nature discovered by scientists, the law of gravity for instance, are simply Allah's way of doing things, and Allah is free to break or change them at will. Why Allah does things this way and not another is not for us to know.

Today's Muslim scientists are still reluctant to challenge this belief. Pervez Hoodbhoy, professor of physics at Quaid-i-Azam University in Islamabad, Pakistan, writes that "When the 2005 earthquake struck Pakistan, killing more than 90,000 people, no major scientist in [Pakistan] publicly challenged the belief, freely propagated through the mass media, that the quake was God's punishment for sinful behavior." And he added that "an overwhelming majority of my university's science students accepted various divine-wrath explanations."

Then why study science? Of what use is it? Hoodbhoy writes: "Science, in the view of [Islamic] fundamentalists, is principally seen as valuable for establishing yet more proofs of God, proving the truth of Islam and the Quran."

According to fundamentalist Islamic thinking, the purpose of science is to serve religion. But scientists cannot rely on the Quran for guidance. They must follow the scientific method: formulating problems, collecting facts through observation and experiment, and formulating and testing hypotheses. And they must do all this critically and independently, arriving at conclusions free of any religious authority.

And so we see the clash in the Islamic world between traditional religious thinking and the critical thinking of scientists. To the fundamentalist mindset, any new knowledge the scientist uncovers must coincide with what the Quran says. Scientific knowledge must not contradict the sacred knowledge. For example, scientists have found that humans evolved from chimpanzees. Edis says: "[B]ecause the Quran is fairly explicit about the special creation of humans—Adam and Eve and so forth—you will find that Muslims will typically be very reluctant to allow for human evolution."

Many Christian fundamentalists have a similar opinion about evolution, but scientists in the Western world remain free to pursue their work on evolution. Hoodbhoy writes that for science to have a similar free reign in the Islamic world, Muslims must develop an attitude that "shrugs off the dead hand of tradition, rejects fatalism and absolute belief in authority . . . and respects cultural and personal freedoms." Hoodbhoy is talking about nothing less than an intellectual revolution. "The struggle to usher in science will have to go side-by-side with a much wider campaign to elbow out rigid orthodoxy and bring in modern thought, arts, philosophy, democracy, and pluralism [tolerating a range of differing ideas and opinions]."

Madrassas

For this revolution to take place, the Arab world's educational practices will have to change, and that will not be easy. Islamic fundamentalists strongly oppose non-religious education. They want the subjects taught in secular schools limited to the same ones taught in *madrassas*: Arabic, the Quran and other sacred texts, and Shariah.

Madrassas are fundamentalist religious schools where boys and girls, starting at age nine, are taught mostly about Islamic religion. Madrassas are found in Muslim countries all around the world, with an estimated 20,000 in Pakistan alone, and also in non-Muslim countries with large immigrant populations in Europe, as well as in the United States.

A typical madrassa has two courses of study. The *Hifz* course is dedicated to memorizing the entire Quran. Students typically take three to five years to complete this course. A student who succeeds earns the title of "*Hafiz al-Quran.*" The *Alim* course is a study of Islamic grammar, literature, Shariah, history, and Hadith. An Alim student typically takes six years to finish.

Madrassas are widely regarded as moderate institutions focused on religious education only. Many are dedicated to taking in poor students from rural areas, whose education, room, and board are all paid for by outside donations.

Madrassas have their critics. Pakistani journalist Ahmed Rashid wrote, "Many students develop an intolerant, prejudiced . . . and narrow-minded view of the world." Syed Nomanul Haq, a professor of history at the University of Pennsylvania, stated: "Madrasas [sic] . . . have become politically charged training grounds instead of places of learning." U.S. Secretary of State Colin Powell denounced madrassas as breeding grounds for fundamentalists and terrorists. And Alastair Lawson of the BBC reported that "[m]ost members of the Taleban government overthrown by the Americans following the 11 September, 2001, attacks in the United States had attended madrassas in Pakistan."

Madrassas also have their defenders. Author Peter Bergen and researcher Swati Pandey wrote that "While madrassas may breed fundamentalists who have learned to recite the Koran . . . there is little or no evidence that madrassas produce terrorists capable of attacking the West." In their study on the educational backgrounds of seventy-five terrorists who had participated in attacks on Westerners, Bergen and Pandey found that only nine had attended madrassas. "[T]he idea that madrassas are incubating the next generation of terrorists offers the soothing illusion that desperate, ignorant automatons are attacking us rather than college graduates, as is often the case," they wrote.

Colleges and Universities

Bergen and Pandey's study found that a majority of the seventy-five terrorists investigated were college-educated. This may seem surprising, since Islamic fundamentalists typically look at secular colleges and universities with suspicion. They see them as potentially dangerous institutions in which students are exposed to free expression and Western ways. In a strict Muslim theocracy, this exposure may make both professors and students hungry for personal freedom. Then they may end up demanding that society be modernized and Shariah prohibitions relaxed, though this clearly is not always the case, as Bergen and Pandey's study shows.

Iranian fundamentalists in particular have dealt harshly with the nation's universities and their students. In January 1979 the secular Iranian government was overthrown in a revolution. An Islamic theocracy took its place, and universities soon became the target of fundamentalist reformers who clamped down hard on professors and students who showed signs of becoming Westernized.

In 2007 the ruling Iranian theocracy launched a similar anti-Westernization campaign. Thousands of Iranians in universities and colleges were harassed by Iranian police. Professors and students were threatened, arrested, detained, and interrogated. For example, eight student leaders from Iran's Amirkabir University were jailed after students demonstrated against the government by setting fire to pictures of Iranian President Mahmoud Ahmadinejad.

Hadi Ghaemi is a researcher with Human Rights Watch, an international organization dedicated to protecting the human rights of people everywhere. Ghaemi says that the Iranian president "has repeatedly stated his goal of purging Iranian society of secular thought. This is taking shape as a cultural revolution, particularly on university campuses, where persecution and prosecution of students and faculty are intensifying with each passing day."

This tug-of-war between true believers and their critics continues. Now, a broad look at how Islamic fundamentalists want to remake not only Muslim society, not only the Arab world, but the entire planet.

11
We Must Change the World

To Islamic fundamentalists, the ideal society is a place where their religion, strictly interpreted, provides the foundation for law, education, and culture. And they are dedicated to making this ideal society a reality—not just in their own nation but all around the world.

But they see their ideals met with a great deal of resistance. When they survey the forces confronting them, they see the same three formidable enemies Christian fundamentalists see. Corrupt, false religions can endanger the survival of their true religion. A secular government may interfere with the practice of their religion. And a modernized civil society threatens to confuse and pollute traditional Islamic beliefs and practices. What strategies do they use to defeat these enemies and realize their fundamentalist utopia?

War and Politics

One strategy is military. From 2000 to 2006, 43 percent of the world's civil wars were religious, compared to 25 per-

A SHIITE MUSLIM CLERIC, LEFT, SHAKES HANDS WITH A SUNNI CLERIC IN BAGHDAD, IRAQ, IN 2005 AS RIVAL SHIITE AND SUNNI LEADERS WORK AT DRAFTING A NEW IRAQI CONSTITUTION.

cent in the 1940s and 1950s. And most of the religious civil wars since 1940—thirty-four of forty-two—have involved Islam, including nine that were strictly Islamic, with Muslim sects fighting one another. In 2002 in Iraq, for example, after the United States invaded to depose dictator Saddam Hussein, a civil war broke out between Sunni and Shia factions. Sunnis and Shiites have been rival religious factions for hundreds of years, each claiming to be the one and only true Muslim sect. The goal in a religious civil war is winner take all. Each radical faction attempts to win military control over the entire nation so that it can then totally exclude the defeated faction from power.

Osama bin Laden's Sunni radical group al-Qaeda has a broader military goal in mind. Bin Laden would like to overthrow all secular Muslim governments. In his view they are all corrupt. In the process he would expel all Westerners and non-Muslims from these countries. Then he would eliminate their geographical boundaries, creating a pan-Islamic caliphate, a single Islamic theocracy encompassing the entire Muslim world.

Another strategy for creating a fundamentalist utopia is political. A fundamentalist faction tries to rise to political power in order to eventually transform the entire nation into an Islamic state. In the Middle Eastern nation of Lebanon, for example, the radical Shia group Hezbollah, or Party of God, has become a powerful political movement. Hezbollah's rise to power began with military action. In 1982 Israel had invaded Lebanon, then remained as an occupying force. But in 2000, Hezbollah troops drove the Israelis out and kept them out. Hezbollah has also established valuable social services and health care for the public. By 2007 these accomplishments had gained Hezbollah about 20 percent of the seats in Lebanon's parliament, which is split up among several Christian and Muslim factions. At the present time it is unlikely to happen, but eventually Hezbollah hopes to win enough seats and enough power to transform Lebanon from a secular republic to a fundamentalist Islamic theocracy.

Culture Clashes

Even with an Islamic theocracy in power, the cultural battle remains to be fought. The corrupting influences of Western culture must be defeated. Islamic scholars and journalists use the term "Westoxified"—intoxicated by exposure to Western pop culture—to describe what can happen to Muslims who start picking up the bad habits of Westerners.

Among those bad habits are listening to the pop music or watching the movies and TV programs of Western nations. Fundamentalist Islamic culture has no room for rock 'n' roll or hip hop or *The Simpsons*. In the Pakistani capital of Islamabad in April 2007, followers of fundamentalist cleric Maulana Abdul Aziz took dramatic action against these "Westoxifying" media products.

Pakistan is ruled by a secular government that allows people to buy and enjoy Western-style music and movies. Aziz challenged that government, headed by General Pervez Musharraf, by launching an anti-vice campaign with bonfires in the streets. Thousands of his followers burned Western DVDs and cassettes outside of Islamabad's Lal Masjid, or Red Mosque, and an adjoining madrassa, only a few hundred yards from the city's government district. As the DVDs and cassettes went up in flames, Aziz's followers shouted "God is great!" Addressing a crowd of some three thousand followers at the Red Mosque, Aziz demanded strict enforcement of Shariah law and called for violent jihad to deal with these immoral Western influences.

Similar protests took place in the northwestern part of

the country. In one town some two hundred armed men halted passing automobiles to inspect them. Any cassette players or mobile phones they spotted they ripped out and smashed. In another town, armed men used explosive devices to destroy music shops.

Moderate Muslims in Pakistan who sharply disagreed with Aziz and his followers let it be known that they did not wish to live in an anti-Western fundamentalist society. Thousands of Muslim moderates staged demonstrations in cities across Pakistan, chanting anti-extremist slogans and demanding that the government crack down on Aziz and his followers and bring a halt to their Taliban-style tactics. One speaker told the crowd, "Concerned citizens have been watching with anger and frustration the terrorism being inflicted on them by the extremist fringe within society." The demonstrators included members of women's rights and human rights groups who carried banners with messages such as "No to religious extremism, yes to life and music."

Oust the Western Occupiers

U.S. President George W. Bush also criticized fundamentalist–inspired anti-Western activities. In an October 2005 speech, he stated: "We know the vision of the radicals. . . . First, these extremists want to end American and Western influence in the broader Middle East, because we stand for democracy and peace and stand in the way of their ambitions." The president then quoted al-Qaeda's leader. Osama bin Laden had called on Muslims to dedicate their "resources, sons and money to driving the infidels out of their lands," Bush said.

President Bush was partly right. Yes, bin Laden did reject Western-style democracy. But in his "Letter to the American People," bin Laden called for Muslims to oust

Embracing Modern Technology

Many Muslims reject Western influences that they believe will corrupt their religion and traditional culture. But that doesn't mean they reject all of Western culture. Even Islamic fundamentalists use the Internet and cell phones, and use is going up. One study found that during 2005, cell phone usage in the Arab world increased by 82 percent.

This technological revolution has prompted Muslims to consult clerics for religious rulings on the proper use of these new devices. Does Shariah law permit cell phone owners to use verses from the Quran as ring tones? Can cell phones be used to summon believers to prayer? Rulings on both these questions resulted in a simple yes.

Answers to other questions can be more complex. Is it permissible to send your wife text messages on your cell phone announcing that you are divorcing her? Traditionally in a Muslim marriage, the man is the only one with the right to call for a divorce. He may divorce his wife by simply announcing to her three times, "I divorce you." But may the husband send the three announcements in the form of a text message over a cell phone to his wife? Yes, an Islamic cleric in Egypt ruled. However, in addition to the text message the husband must also obtain a permanent, written document as proof of his announcement to divorce her.

Cell phones have changed dating habits in the Arab world as well. Shariah law prevents unmarried males and females from being alone together. But now they may get acquainted through private cell phone conversations. Cell phones have changed mating habits as well. A woman in Gaza used her cell phone camera at a neighborhood wedding to take pictures of the unmarried women who attended. Later, she showed the pictures to her unmarried son, who was looking for a mate.

Westerners from Muslim lands for very different reasons: "Your forces occupy our countries; you spread your military bases throughout them; you corrupt our lands . . . to protect the security of the Jews."

Bin Laden was referring to the vital part played by the United States in the long struggle between Israel and the Arab world. In 1948, the state of Israel was created when the United Nations divided the area known as Palestine into separate Jewish and Arab states. Ever since then Muslim nations such as Lebanon and Egypt have been struggling to return Israel's land to Arab control. Their failure to eliminate Israel is in part due to the steady supply of money and arms flowing in to Israel from the United States.

Another reason bin Laden wants to get rid of Western influence is the vast oil reserves in Middle Eastern nations. "You steal our wealth and oil at paltry prices," he says. "This theft is indeed the biggest theft ever witnessed by mankind in the history of the world." In other words, we object to the West's economic, military, and cultural presence in our lands and Western interference in Islamic political affairs.

In May 2006 Iran's president, Mahmoud Ahmadinejad, sent his own letter to President Bush, stating his thoughts on the U.S. president's efforts to bring democracy to the Middle East, beginning with the 2002 invasion of Iraq and its ongoing occupation by U.S. forces. The Iranian president wrote:

Liberalism and Western-style democracy have not been able to help realize the ideals of humanity. Today these two concepts have failed. Those with insight can already hear the sounds of the shattering and fall of the ideology and thoughts of the Liberal democratic systems. . . . Whether we like it or not, the world is gravitating towards faith in the

102

Almighty and justice and the will of God will prevail over all things.

Not surprisingly, bin Laden and Ahmadinejad, both radical Islamic fundamentalists, reject Western-style democracy and pluralism in favor of traditional Islamic theocracy. They are determined that Westerners must be removed from Muslim lands, even if it means using violence to get the job done.

The Quran and Violence

But does the Quran permit the use of violence to remove oppressors and occupiers? Surah 22, verse 39 reads: "Permission (to fight) is given to those upon whom war is made because they are oppressed, and most surely Allah is well able to assist them." In his "Letter to the American People," bin Laden wrote, "It is commanded by our religion and intellect that the oppressed have a right to return the aggression. Do not await anything from us but Jihad, resistance and revenge."

While the Quran does permit violent jihad, it sets certain limits: "[F]ight in the way of Allah with those who fight with you, and do not exceed the limits" (2:189). Do these limits permit the use of suicide attacks, such as those carried out by the nineteen terrorist hijackers in the 9/11 attacks on the United States? The Quran is very clear about *intihar*, the act of suicide. Surah 4, verse 29 expressly forbids Muslims to "kill (or destroy) yourselves." Nor does the Quran permit the killing of noncombatants, innocent people not involved in the fighting, such as the nearly three thousand people killed in the 9/11 attacks.

But Muslims who carry out suicide attacks do not see themselves as committing suicide. They see themselves as martyrs in a holy war, voluntarily enduring death in the name of their religion. And the Quran assures such martyrs a blessed afterlife: "Think not of those, who are slain in the way of Allah, as dead. Nay, they are living" (3:169). And they will "rejoice in the bounty provided by Allah" (3:170).

In a 2007 newspaper interview, a twenty-four-year-old man from Jordan explained why he plans on becoming a suicide bomber: "I want to spread the roots of God on this Earth and free the land of occupiers. I don't love anything in this world. What I care about is fighting." And who shall be his targets? The young man is a Sunni Muslim. "First, the Shiites. Second, the Americans. Third, anywhere in the world where Islam is threatened."

But what about the innocent noncombatants injured and killed in these suicide attacks, such as the nearly three thousand victims of the 9/11 attacks? Muslim journalist Yamin Zakaria is an apologist for—a defender of—Islamic terrorists, whom he calls "freedom fighters." He lives in London, England. "Why should the armed forces be exclusively targeted," Zakaria writes, "when it was the political establishment (civilians) in collusion with the mass media that usually initiates and authorises war? . . . What about the non-combat military personnel like doctors, cooks, cleaners, accountants and nurses? What about the commercial firms that supplies the lethal arms?" In other words, noncombatants also fight—indirectly. "Therefore, the distinction between combatants and noncombatants is blurred in the context of warfare, as substantial sections of civilian life contribute to the war machine." So, to a terrorist there really is no such thing as an innocent noncombatant. When it comes to jihad, all are fair game.

Osama bin Laden said much the same thing in his "Letter to the American People." But he added another justification for the killing of noncombatants: revenge.

Allah, the Almighty, legislated the permission and the option to take revenge. Thus, if we are at-

tacked, then we have the right to attack back. Whoever has destroyed our villages and towns, then we have the right to destroy their villages and towns. Whoever has stolen our wealth, then we have the right to destroy their economy. And whoever has killed our civilians, then we have the right to kill theirs.

Christian Fundamentalists and Violence

Charles Kimball, professor of Comparative Religion in the Divinity School at North Carolina's Wake Forest University, has worked with religious institutions in the Middle East. In an article about faith and violence, he comments on the fundamentalist belief in absolute truth: "People who believe they . . . know what God wants for them have proven time and again that they're capable of doing anything because it's not their will but God's will being carried out." He adds, "You see this most obviously in a suicide bomber—someone who is convinced he or she knows what God wants, and can end up doing the most horrific things to innocent people."

Christian fundamentalists also believe they know the absolute truth and are carrying out God's will as they work to change society. Yet no religious civil wars have broken out in the United States. And aside from a few scattered abortion clinic bombings, very few terrorist attacks have been committed by Christian fundamentalists in the United States. Why not? Religious historian George Marsden points to the American heritage of separation of church and state and individual freedom of choice. "Although [Christian fundamentalists in the United States] believe legislation should reflect God's moral law on selected issues such as abortion or gay marriage," he writes, "their general instinct on most matters is to advocate voluntary persuasion rather than governmental coercion." While Christian fundamentalists very much want society to reflect their religion's moral values, only the most radical favor the Taliban-style approach of policing citizens to make sure they obey religion-based laws. Instead, they work to change their nation's government by electing leaders who share their biblically based values.

Unfair and Unjust?

What else separates Christian fundamentalists living in the United States from Islamic fundamentalists living in the Arab world? Social scientists have created personality profiles of radical Islamic fundamentalists in the Arab world, based on interviews with these men and research into their backgrounds. Valerie J. Hoffman, associate professor for the Study of Religion at the University of Illinois at Champaign-Urbana, examined the results of these studies and found that radical fundamentalists are typically anxious individuals driven by feelings of alienation, inferiority, anger, and resentment.

These feelings can come from living in a developing nation where most people are poor, the results show. Islamic fundamentalists view the relative poverty in the Arab world as unfair and unjust. They see themselves as the virtuous and godly people while Westerners, who enjoy a much higher standard of living, are the immoral and ungodly people. Why, radical fundamentalists wonder, are the godly Muslims like themselves not the ones who are rich in worldly goods instead?

These men feel that the West is to blame. They feel invaded. Christian fundamentalists in the United States have no reason to feel invaded by another nation's culture. But radical Islamic fundamentalists see themselves as victims of Western aggression. Westerners have robbed them of their self-respect and kept them down. Surely Allah must want Muslims to rise up and set things right. In the hearts and minds of many radical Islamic fundamentalists, the only way out of this economic and moral dilemma is jihad, waging holy war against their oppressors.

Many nonfundamentalist Muslims strongly disagree with this kind of thinking. While the world may be unfair and unjust, violence will not make it less so. Wafa Sultan is a Syrian-American psychiatrist living in California. She has been interviewed on Arab television about her views on Muslim holy warriors. Jihad is not the answer, she says, and the people who wage it are not true Muslims. "Muslims must ask themselves what they can do for humankind, before they demand that humankind respect them." She believes that a crucial battle is being waged between fundamentalists and moderates for the soul of Islam: "It is a clash between a mentality that belongs to the Middle Ages and another mentality that belongs to the 21st century. It is a clash between civilization and backwardness, between the civilized and the primitive, between barbarity and rationality."

12
East versus West

In the Arab world Islamic fundamentalists struggle to stem the incoming tide of Western influence and preserve their religious traditions. Other Islamic fundamentalists undergo a different and even tougher struggle, literally surrounded by Western culture. Muslims continue to immigrate to Europe in increasing numbers. As of 2007, an estimated 15 million to 17 million Muslims lived in Europe. The Muslim population of France is the largest in Western Europe, estimated at between five and six million. In France and The Netherlands, Muslims are estimated to make up between and 5 and 10 percent of the total population; in Britain, about 3 percent. Europe's Muslim immigrants must struggle not only to preserve their religious traditions but to cope with the surrounding majority culture.

Meanwhile, the primarily Christian majority populations of these nations must struggle to adapt to the incoming Muslim immigrants. Like the United States, European nations have laid down a wall of separation between church and state. Adultery is not a crime. Homosexuality is accepted. Women may drive cars, vote in elections, and walk about in public unaccompanied and without being covered from head to toe.

Leave Them to Themselves

For the most part, European governments have taken a multicultural approach toward this influx of Muslim immigrants. They advise citizens that, since all cultures and value systems are equal, they must be tolerant and respectful of their new neighbors. Do not criticize the Muslim lifestyle, they are told. It is neither better nor worse, just different.

The problem with this approach, writes Richard Wolin in the *Nation* magazine, is that it does not encourage Muslim immigrants to integrate and become part of their host society: "Instead of assimilating, immigrants have been encouraged to maintain their time-honored, traditional religious and cultural orientations." As a result, they tend to live in poor, overcrowded, segregated neighborhoods—immigrant ghettos, where they remain separate from the host society, feeling like strangers in a strange land. Meanwhile, Europeans also tend to see Muslim immigrants as strangers, treating them with tolerant respect but maintaining their distance. "By encouraging 'difference' among ethnic subgroups," Wolin writes, "multiculturalism ends up turning these groups into targets of resentment and thereby insuring their rejection by the majority culture."

Contacts between cultures are not made. Ideas are not exchanged. Friendships are not built. Critics insist that this well-meaning multicultural brand of tolerance leads to isolation, alienation, and lack of change. It tends to encourage Muslim immigrants to stick to the traditional lifestyle of their Arab homeland. Author Bruce Bawer has lived in The Netherlands and Norway and has traveled through much of Europe, writing about the Islamic immigrants there. In a 2007 television interview, he said:

> **[T]hey have their own schools where the kids are taught the Koran, and Koranic values. And you know, fathers, the patriarchs are able to treat their wives just however they want to. Women have no rights to speak of. Their daughters are sold off in marriages. . . . [T]here's no freedom of speech, there's no freedom of religion. This is the mentality that's been imported into Europe.**

Insulting the Prophet

Many non-Muslim Europeans feel comfortable with this influx of Muslims. Even Christians who are the only non-Muslims on their block say they feel safe and secure. But other non-Muslim Europeans say they feel anxious and uncomfortable living in close proximity to thousands of Muslims who violate what to them are basic human rights.

One of those basic human rights is freedom of speech. On September 30, 2005, a Danish newspaper, the *Jyllands-Posten*, announced that it was publishing a series of political cartoons as part of an ongoing debate on multiculturalism and Islam. The paper thought that Europeans were trying so hard not to offend Muslim immigrants that they were engaging in self-censorship—violating their own precious tradition of freedom of expression. So the *Jyllands-Posten* published a dozen political cartoons depicting Muhammad in ways meant to comment critically on the Prophet of Islam. In one cartoon, for example, Muhammad wears a turban shaped like a bomb, complete with burning fuse: the Prophet as Islamic terrorist. The cartoons were shown in other newspapers and on television worldwide.

**FRENCH MUSLIMS PROTEST CARTOONS DEPICTING PROPHET MUHAM-
MAD IN EUROPEAN NEWSPAPERS IN 2006. THEIR "L'ISLAMOPHOBIE"
BANNER REFERS TO ISLAMOPHOBIA, THE FEAR AND DISLIKE THAT
SOME EUROPEANS OPENLY HOLD TOWARD MUSLIM IMMIGRANTS.**

Shariah law sets down many prohibitions, and one of
the most sensitive involves freedom of expression. Islam
absolutely forbids picturing Allah or Muhammad in any
form whatsoever, and violating this prohibition constitutes
a sin so dire that Allah will never forgive it.

Fundamentalist-minded Muslims saw the cartoons as
an unforgivable insult directed at the Prophet Muhammad
—an attack on Islam—and responded accordingly. Outraged demonstrators gathered in Europe, Asia, and
the Arab world. Thousands protested the cartoons in
Lebanon, Pakistan, Iraq, Syria, Iran, Afghanistan, Indonesia, India, and England. In London, demonstrators held up
signs declaring: EXTERMINATE THOSE WHO MOCK ISLAM

and BE PREPARED FOR THE REAL HOLOCAUST. Eventually, things turned violent. In Damascus, Syria, demonstrators set fire to the Danish embassy, chanting, "With our blood and souls we defend you, O Prophet of God."

Nonfundamentalists React

Westerners saw the cartoons in a very different light. Author and columnist Andrew Sullivan wrote: "Should non-Muslims respect this taboo? I see no reason why. You can respect a religion without honoring its taboos. . . . If violating a taboo is necessary to illustrate a political point, then the call is an easy one. Freedom means learning to deal with being offended."

Sullivan's point about Muslims living in today's world is a crucial one. Chances are they will be offended now and then by what appears in newspapers and on television, but in a globalized world everyone must learn to live with words and images that offend them.

Westerners must also stand ready to defend their freedom of expression in a globalized world. Ibn Warraq was born to Muslim parents in India and was schooled in madrassas in Pakistan. Today he is a scholar of Islam living in Europe and best-selling author of *Why I Am Not a Muslim*. "Freedom of expression is our Western heritage and we must defend it or it will die from totalitarian attacks," Warraq writes. "[Freedom of expression] is also much needed in the Islamic world. By defending our values, we are teaching the Islamic world a valuable lesson, we are helping them by submitting their cherished traditions to Enlightenment values." That is, by exercising the Western tradition of freedom of expression to comment on Muslim traditions, Westerners are teaching Muslims a lesson in democracy: that religious traditions are not sacred to everyone, that they can be looked at in a critical light.

Many Muslims did not take this lesson to heart. Instead, they angrily demonstrated their intolerance for Western criticism of traditional Islamic values. Bawer comments: "[M]ulti-culturalism works if the cultures . . . respect basic human rights. . . . If you're dealing with a culture that is essentially intolerant of other values, and that is oppressive itself, then multi-culturalism causes problems."

Women Oppressed

Muslim immigrants in Europe have also held closely to traditional Islamic values that regulate the treatment of women. Ayaan Hirsi Ali was born in a Muslim family in the East African nation of Somalia and grew up in Africa and Saudi Arabia. She was twenty-three in 1992 when her family decided that she must marry a distant cousin she had never met, a Muslim man who, in her words, would have reduced her to being his slave. So Ayaan fled as a refugee to The Netherlands, where she expected to live a life free of the oppressive restrictions of Muslim family life.

But Ayaan found that even in a free society, Muslim women were not free. Muslim men had brought those oppressive restrictions along with them to Europe, determined to keep girls and women from becoming Westernized. Many Muslim girls were either pulled out of school or were sent back to their traditional homeland to be educated in madrassas. And so they would not learn the language and customs of their new country. Muslim women were still subject to arranged marriages to men they had never met, brought over from their traditional homeland. And living in their immigrant ghettos, they were still subject to the traditional dress codes and other Shariah restrictions. Ayaan wrote that life for a woman in a Muslim community in The Netherlands was like living in two cages at once: "Women and girls are locked up in the inner cage, but surrounding this is a larger cage in which the entire Islamic culture has been imprisoned."

Ayaan escaped those cages by learning Dutch, working as an interpreter, and earning a university degree. She then went into politics and served as a member of the Dutch parliament from 2003 to 2006. During that time she worked to strengthen the rights of Muslim women in Europe. In 2005, *Time* magazine named her one of the 100 Most Influential People of the year. Ayaan Hirsi Ali continues to champion Muslim women's rights today.

Men Radicalized

And what about Muslim men who have immigrated to Europe? The majority have been law-abiding citizens. But a few fundamentalist jihadists have done a great deal of damage. Since 9/11, they have been involved in murders, riots, and bombings committed in the name of jihad.

In 2004, for example, Dutch filmmaker and newspaper columnist Theo Van Gogh was shot to death in broad daylight and then mutilated on the streets of Amsterdam, The Netherlands capital. The killer was Mohammed Bouyeri, the son of Moroccan immigrants. Working with Ayaan Hirsi Ali, Van Gogh had made *Submission*, a short film about the abusive treatment of women in Islamic societies, which had recently been shown on Dutch television. In a television interview, Van Gogh said the film was "intended to provoke discussion on the position of enslaved Muslim women. It's directed at the fanatics, the fundamentalists." Bouyeri's five-page note left with Van Gogh's mutilated body identified him as an Islamic jihadist who had killed the journalist and filmmaker as an act of revenge for his attacks on Islam. The note ended this way: "I know for sure that you, O America, are going to meet with disaster. I know for sure that you, O Europe, are going to meet with disaster. I know for sure that you, O Holland, are going to meet with disaster."

Also in 2004, in Madrid, Spain, terrorists set off bombs in the subway system, killing nearly two hundred people and wounding more than two thousand. The Spanish courts laid the blame on an al-Qaeda inspired terrorist group. Jamal Zougam, a Moroccan Muslim, was found guilty of helping to carry out the attack.

In 2005, a series of coordinated bombs detonated the London, England, public transportation system. Three subway trains were hit within fifty seconds of each other, and an hour later a bus was hit. Fifty-five people were killed in the attacks and some seven hundred were injured. The four Islamic suicide bombers who carried the explosives were also killed in the blasts.

In 2007, two Muslim men drove a Jeep loaded with gas cylinders and gasoline into the glass doors of the main terminal at the Glasgow, Scotland, International Airport, setting the terminal afire. One was Iraqi doctor Bilal Abdullah, age twenty-seven. The other, Kafeel Ahmed, also twenty-seven, was from Bangalore, India. He held a degree in aeronautical engineering and had studied at universities in Ireland and England. He was believed to be the driver of the Jeep. Ahmed died of burns suffered in the incident. A suicide note found at the scene indicated that both intended to die as martyrs in the terrorist attack.

Islamic terrorists have struck in other European nations as well. Some of the jihadists involved were born and educated in Europe. Some, such as Bouyeri, spoke their host country's language fluently; and some, such as Abdullah, were successful professionals living apparently comfortable, Westernized lives. But these were not comfortable men. They were radical Islamic jihadists willing to commit suicide for their cause.

Some Muslim immigrants in Europe do fit in. The fa-

Mistrust: A Personal Testament

Author and essayist Theodore Dalrymple has spent years in Britain working as a psychiatrist. Some of his patients were Islamic immigrants. He writes:

> One of the most sinister effects of the bombers . . . is that they have undermined trust completely. This is because those under investigation turn out not to be cranks or marginals but people who are either well-integrated into society, superficially at least, or who have good career prospects. They are not the ignorant and uneducated; quite the reverse. . . . Nor are they of one ethnic or national group only: We have had Somali, Pakistani, Arab, Jamaican, Algerian and British Muslim terrorists.

Dalrymple writes that moderate Muslims can do a great deal of good for Britain. But that potential good, he confesses, influences his thinking less than "the harm that a few fanatics can do. . . . The 1-in-1,000 chance that a man is a murderous fanatic is more important to me than the 999-in-1,000 chance that he is not a murderous fanatic." And so, "despite friendly and long-lasting relations with many Muslims, my first reaction on seeing Muslims in the street is mistrust; my prejudice, far from having been inherited or [picked up] early in life, developed late in response to events."

Dalrymple is not comfortable with his prejudice. "History is full of the most terrible examples of what happens when governments and peoples ascribe undesirable traits to minorities, and no decent person would wish to participate in the crimes to which this ascription can give rise." Still, he acknowledges, "it would also be folly to ignore sociological reality." It would be blind, foolish, and dangerous to ignore the indisputable fact that the acts of terrorism committed in Britain have all been committed by radical fundamentalist Muslims.

ther of one of the London terrorist bombers owned two shops, two houses, and drove a new Mercedes automobile. But for these bitter young men, multiculturalism had not worked. They did not belong in this technologically advanced, globalized society because they did not want to belong. They saw themselves as superior to the Westerners around them. They were strong, righteous, moral Muslims blessed by Allah with the final revealed truth, surrounded by weak, directionless, decadent Westerners. Why should they adapt their superior selves to an inferior society that discriminates against them? Instead, they would do what Allah had called them to do. They would strike out at that society in His holy name.

Competing Passions

Radical jihadists make up a tiny percentage of the world's Muslims. But Islam is tightly linked to Westerners' anxieties and fears stemming from terrorist attacks. And that anxious attitude leads to Islamophobia, a persistent suspicion, fear, and dislike of all the world's billion-plus Muslims. A study conducted at the University of Leicester in England showed that shortly after the 9/11 attacks, racist and religious attacks on Muslims in the city of Leicester rose dramatically. Insults were shouted at Muslim women out shopping and children on their way to school. A Muslim man had eggs thrown at him. A Muslim baby was tipped out of a baby carriage. The leader of the study, Dr. Lorraine Sheridan, said, "What is of most concern is that this is happening in Leicester, a leading multi-ethnic city which is supposed to be a model for the rest of [England]." Similar incidents still take place on city streets, in madrassas and mosques, and on college campuses in the United States as well as in Europe, especially following a terrorist attack. It's a vicious circle: Radical fundamentalists' intolerant attitude toward Westerners leads to an anti-Muslim attitude on the part of Westerners.

Looking back at religious fundamentalists, Christian and Islamic, words like intolerant, polarizing, and divisive keep coming to mind. Christian fundamentalists complain that secular society is intolerant of Bible believers, while critics complain that fundamentalists are intolerant of other faiths. Religious civil wars erupt between Sunnis and Shiites and other fundamentalist sects who cannot tolerate one another's existence. Christian and Islamic fundamentalists denounce gay people, doctors that perform abortions, schools that do not teach creationism, and secular governments whose laws are not based on holy scripture. Fundamentalists insist that nonbelievers are bound for Hell unless they accept their faith and their faith only. For fundamentalists in general there is always a battle to be fought, and they stand ready to take up the fight.

Religious extremism is a potentially powerful force in any society, and the words of fundamentalists make a good deal of sense to a great number of people. Since they are convinced that their faith is the one and only true religion, the urge to impose it on everyone else is every true believer's natural duty. After all, fundamentalists proclaim, it is for the good of all that everyone believes as we do. Only then can we all live as God intends for us to live, in a fundamentalist theocratic utopia.

But nonfundamentalists are driven by another kind of urge, the democratic passion to live freely and respectfully in a society where no one religion prevails, where many faiths and worldviews, including agnosticism and atheism, are tolerated. Each side is passionate about its stance. Fundamentalists will continue to battle for their one true faith, while their critics will continue to resist in the name of tolerance and pluralism.

Notes

Chapter 1

p. 5, par. 2, "Toward a Hidden God," *Time*, April 8, 1966, http://www.time.com/time/magazine/article/0,9171,83 5309,00.html

p. 5, par. 3, Andrew Sullivan, "The Year That Religion Learned Humility," *Time*, December 21, 2006, http://www.time.com/time/world/printout/0,8816,1572520, 00.html

p. 8, par. 1, Gabriel A. Almond, Emmanuel Sivan, and R. Scott Appleby, "Fundamentalism: Genus and Species," in *Fundamentalisms Comprehended*, ed. Martin E. Marty and R. Scott Appleby, Chicago, IL: University of Chicago Press, 2004, pp. 401–414.

p. 8, par. 3, Margot Patterson, "The Rise of Global Fundamentalism," *National Catholic Reporter*, NRConline. org, May 7, 2004, http://ncronline.org/NCR_Online /archives2/2004b/050704/050704a.php

Chapter 2

p. 12, par. 1, Harry Emerson Fosdick, *"Shall the Fundamentalists Win?": Defending Liberal Protestantism in the 1920s*, History Matters, June 10, 1922, http://historymatters.gmu.edu/d/5070/

p. 13, par. 1, Harold O. J. Brown, "The Problem of Evil,"

MoodyMagazine.com, *Moody Magazine*, July/August 1966, http://www.moodymagazine.com/articles.php? action=view_article&id=321

p. 13, par.2, Bruce Bawer, *Stealing Jesus: How Fundamentalism Betrayed Christianity*, New York: Three Rivers Press, 1997, p. 7.

p. 14, par. 1, Britt Williams, "The Conversion of Britt Williams," Consuming Fire Fellowship, http://www.consumingfirefellowship.org/Conversion.htm

p. 15, par. 1, Britt Williams, e-mail to author, May 11, 2007.

p. 15, par. 2, Britt Williams, "Consuming Fire Fellowship: Ministries," http://www.consumingfirefellowship.org/Ministries.htm

p. 16, par. 3, Bawer, *Stealing Jesus*, p. 10.

p. 16, par. 4, Susan Jacoby, "God Is Not . . . Well, He's Just Not," *Washington Post*, September 2007, http://newsweek.washingtonpost.com/onfaith/susan_jacoby/2007/09/blank_for_now.html

p. 16, par. 4, Christopher Hitchens, "God Is Not Great," Slate.com, April 26, 2007, http://www.slate.com/id/2165033?nav=tap3

p. 17, par. 1, "Basic Beliefs: The Scriptures," Southern Baptist Convention, http://www.sbc.net/aboutus/basicbeliefs.asp

p. 17, par. 2–p. 18, par. 1, Richard Dawkins, "Why I Am Hostile Toward Religion," beliefnet, http://www.beliefnet.com/story/203/story_20334_1.html

p. 18, par. 2, Rowland Croucher, "Statement of Faith and Practice," John Mark Ministries, http://jmm.aaa.net.au/articles/8057.htm

p. 18, par. 4, Fosdick, "Shall the Fundamentalists Win?" History Matters.

p. 19, par. 2, Bawer, *Stealing Jesus*, p. 320.

p. 20, par. 1, Glenn Scherer, "The Godly Must Be Crazy,"

Grist, October 27, 2004, http://www.grist.org/news/maindish/2004/10/27/scherer-christian/

p. 21, par. 2, Joe Kovacs, "Robertson: Disasters Point to 2nd Coming," WorldNetDaily, October 9, 2005, http://www.worldnetdaily.com/news/article.asp?ARTICLE_ID=46737

Chapter 3

p. 22, par. 1, George M. Marsden, *Fundamentalism and American Culture.* New York: Oxford University Press, 2006, p. 252.

p. 23, par. 4, Christopher Hitchens, "God Is Not Great," Slate.com, April 26, 2007, http://www.slate.com/id/2165033?nav=tap3

p. 24, par. 2, Bruce Bawer, *Stealing Jesus: How Fundamentalism Betrayed Christianity,* New York: Three Rivers Press, 1997, p. 7.

p. 24, par. 4, Mark C. Taylor, "The Devoted Student," *New York Times,* December 21, 2006, http://www.nytimes.com/2006/12/21/opinion/21taylor.html

p. 26, par. 2, Susan Jacoby, "God Is Not . . . Well, He's Just Not." *Washington Post,* September, 2007, http://newsweek.washingtonpost.com/onfaith/susan_jacoby/2007/09/blank_for_now.html

Chapter 4

p. 27, par. 1, George M. Marsden, *Fundamentalism and American Culture,* New York: Oxford University Press, 2006, p. 235.

p. 27, par. 1, David Bay, "False Faith—Sure Sign of the End But Necessary to Achieve New World Order," *The Cutting Edge,* http://www.cuttingedge.org/ce1079.html

p. 28, par. 2, "Falwell Apologizes to Gays, Feminists, Lesbians," CNN, September 14, 2001, http://archives.cnn.com/2001/US/09/14/Falwell.apology/

p. 28, par. 3, "Falwell Apologizes," CNN, September 14, 2001.

p. 28, par. 4–p. 30, par. 1, "Falwell Apologizes," CNN, September 14, 2001.

p. 30, par. 3, "Falwell Apologizes," CNN, September 14, 2001.

p. 30, par. 4, Martin E. Marty and R. Scott Appleby, "Introduction," in *Fundamentalisms Comprehended*, ed. Martin E. Marty and R. Scott Appleby, Chicago, IL: University of Chicago Press, 2004, p. 1.

p. 31, par. 2, Glenn Scherer, "The Godly Must Be Crazy," *Grist*, October 27, 2004, http://www.grist.org/news/maindish/2004/10/27/scherer-christian/

p. 31, par. 4–p. 32, par. 1, Bay, "False Faith," http://www.cuttingedge.org/ce1079.html

p. 32, par. 3, "How Do I Recognize a Cult?" CBN.com, http://www.cbn.com/spirituallife/CBNTeachingSheets/FAQ_cult.aspx

p. 32, par. 3, Bruce Bawer, *Stealing Jesus: How Fundamentalism Betrayed Christianity*, New York: Three Rivers Press, 1997, p. 174.

p. 32, par. 4, Bawer, *Stealing Jesus*, p. 174.

p. 32, par. 5, Edward Frost, "Stealing Jesus, a Sermon," Unitarian Universalist Congregation of Atlanta, http://www. uuca.org/sermon.php?id=52

Chapter 5

p. 33, par. 1, Michael D. Shear, "Gingrich Assails 'Radical Secularism,'" *Washington Post*, May 20, 2007, p. A4.

p. 33, par. 2, "NAACD Information," National Alliance Against Christian Discrimination, http://www.naacd.com/

p. 34, par. 2, Harold O. J. Brown, "The Problem of Evil," MoodyMagazine.com, *Moody Magazine*, July/August 1966, http://www.moodymagazine.com/articles.php?action=view_article&id=321

p. 34, par. 3, Brown, "The Problem of Evil."

p. 35, par. 1, Glenn Scherer, "The Godly Must Be Crazy," *Grist*, October 27, 2004, http://www.grist.org/news/maindish/2004/10/27/scherer-christian/

p. 35, par. 4, Tim LaHaye, "Godless Society," *Atlantic Monthly*, November 2007, p. 46.

p. 36, par. 1, "Buncombe One of N.C.'s Top Counties in Home-Schooling," Associated Press, October 27, 2007, http://www.wral.com/news/state/story/1975210/?print_friendly=1

p. 36, par. 1, Jenefer Igarashi, "The Christian Compass," ChristianHomeschooling.us, September 2, 2007, http://www.christianhomeschooling.us/articles/jenefer igarashi1.html

p. 37, par. 2, Igarashi, "The Christian Compass."

p. 37, par. 4, Igarashi, "The Christian Compass."

p. 38, par. 1, "Student Expectations," Bob Jones University, http://www.bju.edu/prospective/expect/dress.html

p. 38, par. 1, "Student Expectations," Bob Jones University.

p. 38, par. 4, Emmanuel Sivan, "The Enclave Culture," in *Fundamentalisms Comprehended*, ed. Martin E. Marty and R. Scott Appleby, Chicago, IL: University of Chicago Press, 2004, p. 31.

p. 39, par. 3, Andrew Sullivan, *The Conservative Soul: How We Lost It, How to Get It Back*, New York: HarperCollins, 2006, p. 45.

p. 39, par. 3, Sullivan, *The Conservative Soul*, p. 26.

p. 40, par. 2, Jeff Sharlet, "Through a Glass Darkly: How the Christian Right Is Reimagining U.S. History," *Harpers*, December 2006, http://www.harpers.org/archive/2006/12/0081322

p. 40, par. 3, Sullivan, *The Conservative Soul*, p. 91.

p. 41, par. 3, Britt Williams, "Consuming Fire Fellowship: Ministries," http://www.consumingfirefellowship.org/Ministries.htm

p. 41, par. 4. "Heaven or Hell?" Pilgrim Fundamentalist Baptist Press, Inc., http://www.pfbaptistpress.org/11. htm

p. 41, par. 6–p. 42, par. 1, Bruce Bawer, *Stealing Jesus: How Fundamentalism Betrayed Christianity*, New York: Three Rivers Press, 1997, p. 6.

Chapter 6

p. 45, par. 2. Dan Gilgoff, "John McCain: Constitution Established a 'Christian Nation,'" beliefnet, September 2007, http://www.beliefnet.com/story/220/story_22001.html

p. 45, par. 3, Tim LaHaye, "Godless Society," *Atlantic Monthly*, November 2007, p. 46.

p. 45, par. 4, "What They Say About Church-State Separation," Americans United for Separation of Church and State, http://www.ausfv.org/quotes.html

p. 46, par. 2, "Treaty of Peace and Friendship between the United States and the Bey and Subjects of Tripoli of Barbary," issued June 7, 1797, http://www.stephenjaygould.org/ctrl/treaty_tripoli.html

p. 46, par. 4, Mark Lilla, "Coping With Political Theology," Cato Unbound, October 8, 2007, http://www.cato-unbound.org/2007/10/08/mark-lilla/coping-with-political-theology/

p. 48, par. 2, Glenn Scherer, "The Godly Must Be Crazy," *Grist*, October 27, 2004, http://www.grist.org/news/maindish/2004/10/27/scherer-christian/

p. 49, par. 1, Lisa Anderson, "Falwell Saw Law School as Tool to Alter Society," *Chicago Tribune*, May 21, 2007, http://www.chicagotribune.com/news/nationworld/chifif3v91may21,1,7181543.story?coll=chi-news-hed

p. 49, par. 2 Anderson, "Fallwell Saw Law School as Tool."

p. 49, par. 3, William J. Federer, "Jefferson Hated 'Hate

Crime' Legislation," WorldNetDaily, May 2, 2007, http://www.wnd.com/news/printer-friendly.asp?ARTI CLE_ID=55479

p. 50, par. 1, Andrew Sullivan, *The Conservative Soul: How We Lost It, How to Get It Back*, New York: HarperCollins, 2006, p. 237.

p. 50, par. 2, Tim Rutten, *"Head and Heart: American Christianities*, by Garry Wills," *Los Angeles Times*, October 10, 2007, http://www.latimes.com/features/ books/la-et-rutten10oct10,1,4461237.story

p. 50, par. 3, Rutten, *"Head and Heart."*

p. 50, par. 4, Rutten, *"Head and Heart."*

p. 51, par. 2, Timothy Noah, "Jerry Falwell's Hit Parade," *Slate*, May 15, 2007, http://www.slate.com/id/2166 220/

p. 52, par. 2, John Helprin, "Evangelicals, Scientists Join on Warming," FoxNews.com, January 17, 2007, http://www.foxnews.com/wires/2007Jan17/0,4670, EvangelicalsGlobalWarming,00.html

p. 52, par. 3, Helprin, "Evangelicals, Scientists Join on Warming."

p. 53, par. 3, Dylan T. Lovan, "High-Tech Museum Brings Creationism to Life," MSNBC, July 31, 2006, http:// www.msnbc.msn.com/id/14122311/

p. 54, par. 2, Edward O. Wilson, "Can Biology Do Better Than Faith?" *New Scientist*, November 2, 2005, http://www.newscientist.com/channel/opinion/dn8254 .html

p. 55, par. 2, "USA TODAY Gallup Poll Results," *USA Today*, June 7, 2007, http://www.usatoday.com/news/ politics/2007-06-07-evolution-poll-results_n.htm

p. 55, par. 3, Margot Patterson, "The Rise of Global Fundamentalism," *National Catholic Reporter*, NRConline.org, May 7, 2004, http://ncronline.org/NCR_ Online/archives2/2004b/050704/050704a.php

Chapter 7

p. 56, par. 2–p. 58, par. 1, Osama bin Laden, "Full Text: bin Laden's 'Letter to America,'" *Observer Worldview*, November 24, 2002, http://observer.guardian.co.uk/world/2002/nov/24/theobserver

p. 58, par. 3, "Falwell Apologizes to Gays, Feminists, Lesbians," CNN, September 14, 2001, http://archives.cnn.com/2001/US/09/14/Falwell.apology/

p. 59, par. 2, "In God's Name," CBS, December 23, 2007, http://alpha.cbs.com/specials/in_gods_name/bios/faiths_represented.php

p. 60, par. 3, "The Noble Qu'ran," USC-MSA Compendium of Muslim Texts, http://www.usc.edu/dept/MSA/quran/

p. 60, par. 4, "Full Text of Iraqi Constitution," *Washington Post*, October 12, 2005, http://www.washingtonpost.com/wp-dyn/content/article/2005/10/12/AR2005101201450.html

p. 63, par. 2, BBC Team, "Sharia," BBC, http://www.bbc.co.uk/religion/religions/islam/beliefs/sharia_print.html

p. 60, par. 4, "The Constitution of Afghanistan," Afghanistan Online, http://www.afghan-web.com/politics/current_constitution.html#preamble

p. 64, par. 2, Daniel Brogan, "Al Qaeda's Greeley Roots," *5280: Denver's Mile High Magazine*, June/July 2003, http://www.5280.com/issues/2003/0306/index.php

p. 64, par. 4, Brogan, "Al Qaeda's Greeley Roots."

Chapter 8

p. 69, par. 1, Matthew Quirk, "Bright Lights, Big Cities," *Atlantic Monthly*, December 2007, p. 32.

p. 71, par. 3, "Fatwa Allows Muslims to Pray Just Three Times a Day," Sunni Forum, October 10, 2007, http://www.sunniforum.com/forum/showthread.php?p=238137

p. 71, par. 4, p. 74, par. 1, Andrew Hammond, "Saudi Fatwa Against Liberals Raises Fears of Violence," *Reuters*, July 8, 2007, http://www.reuters.com/article/latestCrisis/idUSL08171837

p. 72, par. 1, Andrew Sullivan, *The Conservative Soul: How We Lost It, How to Get It Back*, New York: HarperCollins, 2006, p. 256.

p. 74, par. 5–p. 75. par. 1, James Arlandson, "Top Ten Reasons Why Sharia Is Bad For All Societies," *American Thinker*, August 13, 2005, http://www.american thinker.com/2005/08/top_ten_reasons_why_sharia_is. html

p. 75, par. 2, "Nigerian Court Frees Woman Sentenced Under Sharia Law," *Newshour Extra*, September 29, 2003, http://www.pbs.org/newshour/extra/features/july-dec03/sharia4_9-29.pdf

p. 75, par. 3, p. 76, par. 1, Arlandson, "Top Ten Reasons."

p. 76, par. 1, "The Situation Room: Transcripts," CNN, November 20, 2007, http://transcripts.cnn.com/TRANSCRIPTS/0711/20/sitroom.03.html

p. 76, par. 2, BBC Team, "Sharia," http://www.bbc.co.uk/religion/religions/islam/beliefs/sharia_print.html

Chapter 9

p. 78, par. 3. "Prophet Muhammad's Last Sermon," USC-MSA Compendium of Muslim Texts, http://www.usc.edu/dept/MSA/fundamentals/prophet/lastsermon.html

p. 80, par. 3, BBC Team, "Sharia," http://www.bbc.co.uk/religion/religions/islam/beliefs/sharia_print.html

p. 80, par. 4, BBC Team, "Sharia."

p. 81, par. 2, Faiza Saleh Ambah, "For Cloaked Saudi Women, Color Is the New Black," *Washington Post*, May 28, 2007, p. AO1.

p. 82, par. 1, BBC Team, "Sharia."

p. 83, par. 2, Phyllis Chesler, "How My Eyes Were Opened to the Barbarity of Islam," *London Times*, March 7,

2007, http://www.spme.net/cgi-bin/articles.cgi?ID=19 26

p. 83, par. 3, Chesler, "How My Eyes Were Opened."

p. 84, par. 4, Wajiha al-Huweidar, "For Saudi Women, Every Day Is a Battle," May 26, 2007, http://soc. mailarchive.ca/culture.usa/2007-05/12606.html

p. 84, par. 5–p. 85, par. 1, al-Huweidar, "Every Day Is a Battle."

p. 86, pars. 1–3, Megan K. Stack, "In Saudi Arabia, a view from behind the veil," *Los Angeles Times*, June 6, 2007, http://www.latimes.com/news/nationworld/z world/la-fg-women6jun06,0,5491632,full.story

Chapter 10

p. 87, par. 1, "Arab Contributions to Mathematics and the Introduction of the Zero," ArabicNews.Com, April 22, 1998, http://www.arabicnews.com/ansub/Daily/ Day/980422/1998042208.html

p. 88, par. 1, Ilias Fernini, "Islamic Science: A Bibliography of Scholars in Medieval Islam," http://faculty.uaeu. ac.ae/ifernini/history.htm

p. 88, par. 2, Steve Paulson, "The Religious State of Islamic Science," Salon.Com, August 13, 2007, http:// www.salon.com/books/feature/2007/08/13/taner_edis/

p. 90, par. 3, Pervez Amirali Hoodbhoy, "Science and the Islamic World—The Quest for Rapprochement," *Physics Today*, August 2007, http://optonline.aip.org/ journals/doc/PHTOAD-ft/vol_60/iss_8/49_1.shtml

p. 90, par 4, Hoodbhoy, "Science and the Islamic World."

p. 91, par. 1, Paulson, "The Religious State of Islamic Science."

p. 91, par. 2, Hoodbhoy, "Science and the Islamic World."

p. 92, par. 3, Alastair Lawson, "Pakistan's Islamic Schools in the Spotlight," BBC, July 14, 2007, http://news. bbc.co.uk/2/hi/south_asia/4683073.stm

p. 92, par. 3, "Hifz Course," Darul Uloom Al Madania:

An Institution of Higher Islamic Education and Secondary School, November 12, 2006, http://www.madania.org/english/hifz_course.php

p. 92, par. 2, "Alim Course," Darul Uloom Al Madania: An Institution of Higher Islamic Education and Secondary School, November 12, 2006, http://www.madania.org/english/aalim_course.php

p. 92, par. 4, Lawson, "Pakistan's Islamic Schools."

p. 92, par. 4, Bilal Tanweer, "Revisiting Madrasas," *The News on Sunday*, May 6, 2007, http://www.jang.com.pk/thenews/may2007-weekly/nos-06-05-2007/dia.htm#2

p. 92, par. 4, Peter Bergen and Swati Pandey, "The Madrassa Myth," *New York Times*, June 14, 2005, http://www.nytimes.com/2005/06/14/opinion/14bergen.html

p. 92, par. 4, Lawson, "Pakistan's Islamic Schools."

p. 92, par. 5, Bergen and Pandey, "The Madrassa Myth."

p. 93, par. 1, Bergen and Pandey, "The Madrassa Myth."

p. 93, par. 2, Bergen and Pandey, "The Madrassa Myth."

p. 94, par. 2, Robin Wright, "Iran Curtails Freedom In Throwback to 1979," *Washington Post*. June 16, 2007, p. A10.

Chapter 11

p. 97, par. 1, Timothy Samuel Shah and Monica Duffy Toft, "Why God Is Winning," *Foreign Policy*, July/August 2006, http://www.foreignpolicy.com/story/cms.php?story_id=3493

p. 98, par. 4, Stephen Graham, "Cleric Sets Up Islamic Court in Pakistan," *Washington Post*, April 6, 2007, http://www.washingtonpost.com/wp-dyn/content/article/2007/04/06/AR2007040600137.html

p. 99, par. 2, "'Mullahgardi Band Karo': Peaceful Rallies Against Violent Mullahs," *Daily Times*, April 20,

2007, http://www.dailytimes.com.pk/default.asp?page
=2007/04/20/story_20-4-2007_pg7_11

p. 99, par. 3, "President Discusses War on Terror at National Endowment for Democracy," Office of the Press Secretary, October 6, 2005, http://www.whitehouse.gov/news/releases/2005/10/20051006-3.html

p. 100, par. 1, "Arab World Witnesses 82 Percent Increase in Cell Phone Use During 2005," Kuna.net, http://www.kuna.net.kw/home/print.aspx?Language=en&DSNO=907957

p. 101, par. 2, "Cell Phones Invade the Arab World," Allbusiness.com, July 27, 2005, http://www.allbusiness.com/middle-east/israel/483377-1.html

p. 102, par. 1, Osama bin Laden, "Full Text: bin Laden's 'Letter to America,'" *Observer Worldview*, November 24, 2002, http://observer.guardian.co.uk/world/2002/nov/24/theobsever

p. 102, par. 3, bin Laden, "Full Text: bin Laden's 'Letter to America.'"

p. 102, par. 4–p. 103, par. 1, Mahmoud Ahmadinejad, "Letter to President George Bush," *USA Today*, May 9, 2006, http://www.usatoday.com/news/2006-05-09-iran-letter.pdf

p. 103, par. 3, bin Laden, "Full Text: bin Laden's 'Letter to America.'"

p. 104, par. 2, Souad Mekhennet and Michael Moss, "In Jihadist Haven, a Goal: To Kill and Die in Iraq," *New York Times*, May 4, 2007, http://www.nytimes.com/2007/05/04/world/middleeast/04bombers.html

p. 104, par. 3, Yamin Zakaria, "Inside the Mind of a Suicide Bomber," *American Daily*, September 6, 2005, http://www.americandaily.com/article/9141

p. 104, par.4–p. 105, par. 1, bin Laden, "Full Text: bin Laden's 'Letter to America.'"

p. 105, par. 2, Deborah Caldwell, "The Problem With

Monotheism," beliefnet, http://www.beliefnet.com/story/125/story_12546_1.html

p. 105, par. 3–p. 106, par. 1, George M. Marsden, *Fundamentalism and American Culture*, New York: Oxford University Press, 2006, pp. 250–251.

p. 106, par. 2, Valerie J. Hoffman, "Muslim Fundamentalists: Psychosocial Profiles," in *Fundamentalisms Comprehended*, ed. Martin E. Marty and R. Scott Appleby, Chicago, IL: University of Chicago Press, 2004, pp. 199–230.

p. 107, par. 2, John M. Broder, "For Muslim Who Says Violence Destroys Islam, Violent Threats," *New York Times*, March 11, 2006, http://www.nytimes.com/2006/03/11/international/middleeast/11sultan.html?

Chapter 12

p. 108, par. 1, Richard Wolin, "Veiled Intolerance," *The Nation*, April 9, 2007, http://www.thenation.com/doc/20070409/wolin

p. 108, par. 1, "Muslims in Europe: Country Guide," BBC, December 23, 2005, http://news.bbc.co.uk/2/hi/europe/4385768.stm

p. 109, par. 3, Wolin, "Veiled Intolerance."

p. 110, par. 1, Bruce Bawer, transcript from interview on *Bill Moyers' Journal*, PBS, May 11, 2007, http://www.pbs.org/moyers/journal/05182007/transcript2.html

p. 112, par. 1, Andrew Sullivan, "Your Taboo, Not Mine," *Time*, February 5, 2006, http://www.time.com/time/magazine/printout/0,8816,1156609,00.html

p. 112, par. 1, "Embassies Burn in Cartoon Protest," BBC News, February 4, 2006, http://news.bbc.co.uk/2/hi/middle_east/4681294.stm

p. 112, par. 2, Sullivan, "Your Taboo, Not Mine."

p. 112, par. 4, Ibn Warraq, "Democracy in a Cartoon," Spiegel Online, February 3, 2006, http://www.spiegel.de/international/0,1518,398853,00.htm

p. 113, par. 1, Bawer, interview, *Bill Moyers' Journal*.

p. 113, par. 3–p. 114, par.1, Johann Hari, "Islam in the West," *Dissent*, Winter 2007, http://dissentmagazine. org/article/?article=752

p. 114, par. 4–p. 115, par. 1, Ronald Rovers, "The Silencing of Theo van Gogh," Salon, November 24, 2004, http://dir.salon.com/story/news/feature/2004/11/24/va ngogh/

pp. 116–117, Theodore Dalrymple, "The Case for Mistrusting Muslims," *Los Angeles Times*, July 8, 2007, http://www.latimes.com/news/opinion/la-op-dalrym ple8jul08,0,5502943.story?coll=la-opinion-rightrail

p. 118, par. 1, Theodore Dalrymple, "The Suicide Bombers Among Us," *City Journal*, Autumn 2005, http://www.city-journal.org/html/15_4_suicide_bomb ers.html

p. 118, par. 3, Dominic Casciani, "UK 'Islamophobia' Rises After 11 September," BBC News, August 29, 2002,http://news.bbc.co.uk/2/hi/uk_news/2223301.stm

p. 118, par. 2–p. 119, par. 1, Sheila Musaji, "Islamophobia: Incidents," *The American Muslim*, February 11, 2007, http://www.theamericanmuslim.org/tam.php/ features/articles/islamophobia_incidents/0013129

All Internet sites were available and accurate as of April 4, 2008.

Further Information

Books

Fridell, Ron. *Terrorism: Political Violence at Home and Abroad*. Berkeley Heights, NJ: Enslow Publishers, 2001.

Landau, Elaine. *Osama bin Laden: A War Against the West*. Brookfield, CT: Twenty-First Century Books, 2002.

Marguiles, Phillip. *Turning Points in World History—The Rise of Islamic Fundamentalism*. Farmington Hills, MI: Greenhaven Press, 2005.

McGowen, Tom. *The Great Monkey Trial: Science Versus Fundamentalism in America*. New York: Franklin Watts, 1990.

Ruthven, Malise. *Fundamentalism: A Very Short Introduction*. New York: Oxford University Press, 2007.

Wilkinson, Phillip. *Christianity*. New York: DK Children, 2006.

Web Sites

These Web sites are good places to pick up information on the people, places, and ideas in this book.

The Southern Baptist Convention
www.sbc.net/
The official Web site of the United States' largest Protestant fundamentalist group. See the section titled "Basic Beliefs" for a concise rundown of fundamentalist beliefs.

The Young Earth Creation Club
www.creationists.org/
A site dedicated to creation science, giving creationism's side of the evolution debate. Includes links to other pro-creation science sites.

USC-MSA Compendium of Muslim Texts
www.usc.edu/dept/MSA/
A collection of sacred Muslim texts, including the Quran, the Sunnah, and Hadith. Site also has essays explaining various aspects of Muslim culture.

Ijtihad: A Return to Enlightenment
www.ijtihad.org/
This site, dedicated to "freedom of thought and independent thinking among Muslims everywhere," gives the liberal Muslim position on various issues, including terrorism, democracy, and women's rights.

Religious Tolerance
www.religioustolerance.org/
Dedicated to religious freedom, this site deals with the full diversity of religious belief in North America. It also includes information on agnosticism and atheism as well as current religious/political issues such as abortion and same-sex marriage.

BibleGateway.com
www.biblegateway.com/
The Christian Bible in fifty versions and thirty-five languages, all fully searchable.

Bibliography

Bawer, Bruce. *Stealing Jesus: How Fundamentalism Betrayed Christianity*. New York: Three Rivers Press, 1997.

———. *While Europe Slept: How Radical Islam Is Destroying the West from Within*. New York: Doubleday, 2006.

Brown, Wendy. *Regulating Aversion: Tolerance in the Age of Identity and Empire*. Princeton, NJ: Princeton University Press, 2006.

Gorenberg, Gershom. *The End of Days*. New York: Oxford University Press, 2000.

Hecht, Jennifer Michael. *Doubt: A History*. San Francisco: HarperSanFrancisco, 2004.

Lindsey, Hal, with C.C. Carlson. *The Late Great Planet Earth*. Grand Rapids, MI: Zondervan, 1970.

Marsden, George M. *Fundamentalism and American Culture*. New York: Oxford University Press, 2006.

Marty, Martin E., and R. Scott Appleby, eds. *Fundamentalisms Comprehended*. Chicago, IL: University of Chicago Press, 2004.

Nafisi, Azar. *Reading Lolita in Tehran: A Memoir in Books*. New York: Random House, 2003.

Peretti, Frank E. *This Present Darkness*. Wheaton, IL: Crossways Books, 2003.

Sullivan, Andrew. *The Conservative Soul: How We Lost It, How to Get It Back*. New York: HarperCollins, 2006.

Qutb, Sayyid. *Milestones*. Indianapolis, IN: American Trust Publications, 1991.

The Fundamentals: A Testimony to the Truth. http://www.xmission.com/~fidelis/

The Holy Bible.

The Noble Quran. http://www.usc.edu/dept/MSA/quran/

Index

Page numbers in **boldface** are illustrations, tables, and charts.

About the Author

Ron Fridell has written for radio, TV, newspapers, and textbooks. He has written books on social and political issues, such as terrorism and espionage, and scientific topics, such as DNA fingerprinting and global warming. His most recent book for Marshall Cavendish Benchmark was *Prisoners of War* in this series. He taught English as a second language while a member of the Peace Corp in Bangkok, Thailand. He lives in Tucson, Arizona, with his wife Patricia and his dog, an Australian Shepherd named Madeline.